To Ann·Marie —
Thanks for introducing
me to your ark of
Poets!

Best wishes

Philip Wills
10·10·06

the firebridge

Philip Wells

Vernon Harcourt

Whoever speaks in primordial images speaks
with a thousand voices... he transmutes our
personal destiny into the destiny of mankind
and evokes in us those beneficent forces that
ever and anon have enabled humanity to find
a refuge from every peril and to outlive
the longest night

JUNG

Philip Wells appears as The Fire Poet everywhere
from 11 Downing Street to children's hospices, from
maximum security prisons and mental institutions
to nursery and hospital schools, from Warwick
Castle and St. Paul's Cathedral to Eton College
and The Brixton Fridge. This is a selection of poems
from 1995 to 2005.

www.thefirepoet.com

Published by
THE VERNON HARCOURT PRESS
65 Mattock Lane
London W13 9LJ

Designed by Panoram
Front Cover illustration by Darren Hopes

Printed and bound in England by
Biddles Ltd, King's Lynn

To my darling Elizabeth and Laurence

ACKNOWLEDGMENTS

Many thanks to the editors of the following publications
for first printing some of these poems:

*Acumen, Blade, Caduceus, Outposts, Magma, Resurgence,
Fire, Wire, Staple, The Interpreter's House, Urthona, Iota,
Psychopoetica, Doors, New Hope International, Kindred
Spirit, Exile, Aireings, Rustic Rub, The Arcadian, Tears In
The Fence, City Writings, Poems On The Buses, Tandem,
Candelabrum, Poetry Nottingham, Poetry Monthly, Haiku
Quarterly, First Time, Purple Patch*

"Jinja" and "The Pool" also appeared in Earth Songs (ed.
Peter Abbs, Green Books 2002)

A massive thanks to all the people who have kept
listening, supporting, inspiring and encouraging me,
especially Peter Abbs and his metaphysical thrust, Joy
and Fiona for seeing the spark, Tina and her intuitive
gems, Ann for bringing the stars down, Tascha for
believing way beyond the call, Becky for expanding it at
every turn, Daddy, Sonia, Zandra, Simon and Caroline for
enthusing, videoing, megaphoning, loving and praising,
David for fabulous creativity and generosity of heart, Abe
for being a huge light and an amazing friend, Elizabeth
and Laurence for their exquisite, pivotal love and for
putting up with all the faff and froth and guff of Daddy
Volcano, Ang for everything and for editing my life, all
my collaborators-in-art, particularly Sirish, Stephen
Barlow, Hugo Grenville, Steve B-K, Hugo Gerrard, Tracy
and David, and to all the children, who have taught me
immeasurably more than I knew, and last but by no
means least, to William Sieghart, for quietly moving
mountains.

O what Power
Pours a Sun

Into the Hidden Heart
Of Everyone?

CONTENTS

I Treasure In The Rain

II   In The Music Of The Garden

III Horse Whispering In The Military Industrial Complex

I Treasure In The Rain

*There is more wisdom in one drop
of water than in all the books ever
written*
RICHARD JEFFERIES

*The Universe seems wonderful in
theory, but in practice I don't
think it will ever work*
ASHLEIGH BRILLIANT

Creators

Neatly placed on their appointed shelves,
Prize vegetables glitter like crown jewels.
As if they'd grown the bloody things themselves,

Owners of bulbous marrows measure their lives
By volume, width and weight.   What fools.
Neatly placed on their appointed shelves

Sprouts assume a pride outside their little selves:
Another purple-veined face gloats and drools -
As if they'd grown the bloody things themselves!

Whatever time or pesticides this prize involves,
Something's forgotten in the winning and the rules.
Neatly placed on their appointed shelves,

First and second onion inflame the blood, the wives
Exchanging poison recipes then kicking like mules
As if they'd grown the bloody things themselves.

So doctors are Gods when the patient survives;
And designer babies, spliced by researchers' tools,
Neatly placed on their appointed shelves -
As if they'd grown the bloody things themselves.

Falling Apart

Batman? Gandhi? Bruce Willis? Jesus? Superman?
Never showed up. Innocence crushed in a million tons of ash
And not a phoenix to be seen. Only a flying great white shark
With teeth of fire and blood, cloned for destruction
In the blackhole egos of the wounded
Where beauty is smothered in suffocating darkness.

Three thousand hearts torched and torn in hellfire,
Smashed by a hundred floors of ash-thundering steel and stone.

But some, they jumped - some, hand in hand -
Dreaming they might wake before they hit the ground.
They hit the ground. Felt the nightmare concrete punch of dust.

Spiderman? Jesus? No sign. No miracle airlock rescue.
No mother and son reunited in great hug of hope....Hope...

Hope is a candle, burning inside, now spinning in whirlwinds
Of light as supernova hearts explode open at the edge of the universe
And here on earth simultaneously; incredible miracle of the possible,
Light you don't get burned by, to become the sun in your inner sky
And scorch to shame those who think they've found the flame -
They're playing the old, cold game of nail the lovers down.

God forgive them for they know what they do
Father forgive them for they know not what they do

And a light uncurls this fist to a palm as we remember
We are in good hands - the only hands that will hold us forever
With the tenderness always of a newborn in the strong grip
Of his weeping father - the hand that will be there waiting for you
Taking away the pain of your fall

As two ordinary superheroes jump out of burning hell
To know the brief wild freedom of leaving
Their slowmotion skyscraper life hand in hand

Just to open the eyes of the whole world
And show that only love holds us together.

3

The Storm Of Creation

Thunder.
Two continents
of rock collide.

Lightning.
A crack
in the eggshell sky.

Rain.
Cleansing
for the sacrifice.

She cuts off your mind
with a golden sword

and to the drum
of the infinite drum

you hatch
in the healing moss;

and dried
by the lovelight of suns

you fly beyond
the outer skies

to explode
your star of love,

sending out
the storm of your seed

to wake new wings
to the highest skies of fire.

4

Jinja

Though the boys selling Coke at Jinja,
the source of the Nile, have never heard of Egypt,
kingfishers know to point their bills like telescopic
sights and dive; emerge with silver in their beaks,
and the perfume of the Nile in their feathers.

At the river's edge, above the stagnant pool,
red dragonflies advertise their passion;
ignore the disappointment of water
burned to dust at the margins,
never to flow on the great journey.

Flies bright as rubies
move in binary waves
across the river's silver plains:
moving to the rhythms of their race,
if they pierce the river's veil, they drown.

What watches me, beyond the veil?
What watches all the rivers
gliding through my heart?
At the end of my journey,
what sea, what planet waits for me?

In the kayak of my mind I set off
with the faith of horizons, not knowing
what rapids or falls of fire I face, or what
canyons and chasms, what echoes
in what dried-out beds await.

Yet I hear only the rivers and seas turning their wheel;
sense this is no time to question the wisdom
of water, nor the source of all that flows.
I only know these eyes, the sudden dive -
the joy of flight with silver in my beak.

The River Mole

Pretty cygnet nursery -
Mother father swan -
Are happy old bygones;
The better times have gone.

Grafitti spray is cursing the brown bridge:
FUCK RULES on damp concrete.
The damselfly lives for four days.
Just mates and dies.

Look beyond to the arch,
A Victorian dream: bricks
Curving and curling like ferns.

The spiral of a snail rests
On the leaf of a nettle -
Rivers curve through
The landscape of a dock leaf -

And here is the River Mole,
Digging through my unbelief.

I'm digging blind, my pen for claws,
Scratching through earth,
Through Cable TV wires
And buried traffic cones.

The summer bridge takes us
From unknowing to unknowing -
Starflowers drift by and the galaxies
Have better places to go:
I wish it would snow -
And it has...

Slabs of ice are floating down
The river highway
As swallows bell and martins turn
And there is so much more to learn

To be the turning in, so much to earn
To be the burning in, so much to be
To be the longing in -

And snow belonging in me -

I am back to the white fields
And the winter will give way,
And the winter *is* a way

As the flame is a dream you listen in,
The River Mole a theme
To flow beyond the flood of time

To the rippling winds in the buttercup fields -

The wide, wild meadow
Where the other sky waits
To fold you up
Like a flame in the sun.

Old Springs

With the woman in white on his back
the dragon flies through mists of ice
to a sudden campfire, a dark tunnel
and a great fall, ending as the world opens
to a darker version of itself, a cave
hatching to midnight blue
as a switch clicks inferno.

You fly through fire and you are an evening sun
shining on the meeting waters, lighting up
the gold among the pebbles.
A mist of grace smudges the hard lines
of the circling cliffs, where organ pipes
now clarify themselves and groan
before three sopranos from Orion
hurl down a lightning note, and your fingers
are swords cutting through the knots
of ancient texts: a unicorn beats its wings
on your breath; the old springs are chuckling.
The cathedrals of your age are
salt in an unwatched hourglass.

Listen to the beating of anvils
like submarine hatches slamming:
feel the spray of sparks -
Guy Fawkes whispers on Parliament Hill -
as the goddesses swoop
to gather up their new swords:
there will be hatchings in all dimensions;
wings of oil will struggle through the night
before wind and waters return the feathers
as the towered cities of money fall
and a new choir sings over the dust, its music
raining down like the flood, cutting fresh rivers
through the tired land as the soil learns
once more that breaking is an opening

as the broken man kneels and cups his hands
in the pool where all the rivers meet,
breaking the veil for an instant to drink his fill.

The Breath Between

Two continents
rub their cliffs together
like lips.

In the crush of seams
mountains rise
stiff as flutes.

I am the walking in between,
the mountain path
where four winds sing.

I am the hand at the altar
where you speak your heart
and mind and silence...

You look up:
your dance of prayer
has woven into rope:

pull it down now
and hear the iron tongue beat
against the bell of your skull

sending out its sound
in sonic circles,
echo-locating the listeners

who now hear the continents
rubbing their cliffs together
like the lips of a soprano.

Sunday Morning

The things that go without saying -
The nothing-to-heal epiphanies of mornings
At home that leave the busy mind silent:
She's having a mad half hour to Kate Bush,
Our little boy in her arms, and he's laughing
Like the first time laughter broke the sky,
Giggling a rapture we never taught him
Because he's still dripping silver
From the first sacred stream -

He's not solemn or mannered or trying too hard.
My little boy is just giggling in his mother's arms:
And now they're face to face, cheeks on the floor,
And she's crying to *Moments Of Pleasure*
And he points at her tears and exclaims,
With all the freshness of a toddler rolling
His tongue around the juice of a new word:
WET!   And she cries a little more,
For the things that are left without saying.

To Change

Entertainment's doing us in; coin after coin,
Pizza and Playstation, we fritter our gifts;
Ignore the cries for a flipside shift.

And so fear seeps in to numb and dull as time
Turns us from spring to corruption-slime.
The chemical smog hangs and will not lift:

There is nothing we have not interfered with.

And so we ridicule wings, the sense of sublime -
All is lottery and innuendo, lifestyle prying;
TV makeovers where nothing actually changes.

It's all so cowardly: *why are you even trying?*
Castrated voices whine: then I see the Ganges,
Golgotha, Damascus, The Dalai Lama, Beijing:

Tiananmen boys facing the tanks like angels.

London Eye

London Eye wheeling -
   Lambeth Bridge. Charing Cross. Canary Wharf.
     And I am - and you are - evolution reeling -
      Evolution? Mevolution!
Upwardly mobile-phoney/ each virtual man for himself/
     Spinning in the winning treadmill/
STOP THE dotcom-mishmashmemesh-insectocutor CITY

      For the still true

As a cormorant dives beneath Westminster bridge
   In the slowmo flow of new mother Thames -

     The slow eye of the wheel
     Sees through the City screen -

Commuters open their weekend hearts   like peonies

And Telecom Tower's all ears
   To the Whispering Gallery of the cathedral   within

    As I alight the Eye
    Alight with bonfire morning sky -

Big Ben melting in bellsong
Like Dali's clock

And the golden memorial wings
Of the eagle across the water

    Lest we forget

   That I am - and you are -

     Revolution -

      London's inner life
      Turning

        To the burning heart.

The Cry Of Prometheus' Brother

We could have been the great firecliff-and-sea, diving-and-pearl
adventure, from the bullrush source of the musical word to the rapids
thrashing like crocodiles and the hammerheads feasting in frenzy in the
splinters of the sun, waves like cathedrals smashing into the pillars of the
temples of the edge or somewhere a suncloud in a puddle on a high pilgrim
path and the song of the blood like mercury - and not the daily ripping-
out of my brother's charred insides, my own blood, my brother, who always
hid the scream of the iron bird on his tongue, who stole the feathers of the
fire before they ever flew, raped our lady of the high tree like a chainsaw
and cursed me as cowardly as I stood in the steel-seeded cratered fields of
blood and ash with the scars of his darkness in my fists, naked without the
gold he spent and stole from me, from all of us - without the love the fire
was meant to be in the first days we were together before we were parted
and scattered across the black land far from the songs of the sun and the
sea; and the great adventure we swore we would take into the radiance of
the deep has come to the still standing of us in remembrance in the mud
and mist of a darkening village green, each with a white feather in his
hand, and not a dragon or a phoenix or a dove to be seen.

Memory Tree

Bold words unsigned, head-high
inside the hollow oak on the heath:
thick splats of red paint, dried in drips.

In winter matchlit shadows
I read them out to you:
TO THE MEMORY OF MY UNBORN CHILD.

We walked on, lingering
at the carved declarations
of love on the beech's trunk.

Far from the heath I watched
the spring hills swelling, marvelled
at a young oak hugged tight with bark:

suddenly I saw her tears,
and the red paint mournful as spilt blood
lit up by her solemn candle

and her praying inside the oak's empty womb
as ritual blood and ritual light
knitted their healing around her:

easing her pain I hope, the oak
wrapping her up in its grace
like the first mother.

Blow Up The Dam

Blow up the dam, release
the living streams of language!

A trickle of syllables soon
swells into the rhythm of the rivers,
roars in a flood of mind down
to the ancient truth of seas.

Plunge into the seas beyond -
pour the cycles of water and fire
onto the page, into your throat -
blow up the dam that separates
you from me, who are one skull,
woven in a perfect web of gold.

Release the living streams of light!
dive into the oceans of this world -

tend to the unwashed hands,
the tenderness of the predator -
swim naked with the porpoise,
sing in the cathedrals of the sharks -
pulse, like the squid, with all the spectrum

and you, who lived half your life
in the desert beneath the dam,
who feared the little drop of you
would evaporate in fire

are now one mighty sea

clinging tight to the face
of the planet you love.

Piety

You smeared your soul in blood
Enslaved by minds of wire,
But now the fields begin to flood
You listen to the primal fire.

You see the snakes entwine the spires,
The attics white with stars:
You laugh at all the old desires,
Watch goldfish swim through sunken cars

As love rains down its seas to rust
This graveyard greed of steel -
In time for you to reap the dust
And remember how to kneel.

Panma

There was a room in my house
I'd never been to
And my grandfather was there.

It had high ceilings
And sparkled like a cabaret.

He entertained us
With witty rhythms
From the throne of his piano stool.

I was so thrilled to see him.
I had to remind my wife
That he had died.

His every word was a blessing.
It was bliss to hear the stern man
Laugh and sing like a child.

I told him his house and gardens
Were in good hands
And he wept for his father.

We hugged for the first time.
He was frail as bone china,
But wanted *me* to be comfortable.

Waking robbed me
Of his smiling moustache
And deep, unhurried voice.

Then I heard it once more:
Build from the inner life.

There was a room in my house
I'd never been to
And my grandfather was there.

Following

If I am killed, do not assume
That life has lost its innocence;
If my nerves or cells cannot resume
Their work, do not take offence.

I always knew how brief we are,
So learned the patterns of the Sun:
Was there ever any blazing star
Not framed by dark? There is none.

We curse ourselves who curse the world
Where love awaits, and silken days:
I saw the spider's magic pearled,
An abacus of hidden ways -

Love lay beneath my fears and schemes;
Even now I follow, weaving through my dreams.

Even As I Curse

She who fangs the great white
Instructs the larval wasps
To eat the ladybird alive.

And she who lights the stars
Riddles our bodies
With suicidal cells.

She who plants in holy men
The golden seed of labyrinths
Silts the rivers with bones.

And she who embroiders
The fantasies of a child
Clamps its windpipe with her vice.

She who confuses us
Shows us a path.

She who abandons us
Finds us a home.

She who teaches us
Tears us apart.

She who I do not understand
Understands me.

She who loves me,
Even as I curse,
Moves this trembling hand.

Come With Me

with thanks to Francesca Beard

All those for whom bread
Always lands butter side up
When demonstrating Sod's Law -

All those who have ever been torn,
Who still walk between
The fragments with longing

Come with me

All those who've ever felt
Like pigs who've crashed
And burned on the runway

All those who lay themselves down
Across the invisible rivers
Like bridges

20

Skenfrith

Primrose and buttercup
Are satellite dishes in the sun:

Thistle signposts are sharp
As drycleaners' pins.

Hedges bulge with minaret buds:
Bramble-spikes curve like sharkfins.

Hornet spaceships hover
Over wasps drunk among thorns.

A coil of sheepfluff trembles
On a steel barb in the wind.

A cabbage white stutters in,
A screaming mime of wings.

The sky burns with feathers.

Meeting Ted Hughes

His hands are henges
Cupping the secrets of power,
Or a chalice of still water
After Niagara -
The standing stone fingers
Hold the pen between them
Like lightning, as earth and heaven
Battle in storms of rune and glyph.

Red braces stream
From his escarpment shoulders
Like pain
Or a crusader's banner
Hanging from a high ceiling,
Witness to all the creatures
Of blood and the sacrament
Of salmon light.

Measure his voice
On the Richter scale!
It is a mountain moving
The lines of the earth

Shaking the pillars
Of temple and cathedral
To return to the prayer
Of first rock and first light
Where the new time
Of an old art begins
With each heart
Walking the line

Through the henge
Of a sacred hand -
As the falling silver stream
Carves through ancient rock -
As we walk between the stones,
Along the aisle of fire,
Back to the source
Of the singing dawn.

The Academy

They made words and sense here:
Orders and borders and morals and fear.
Not fetres or beat and rimmonsom chims
Or litanies plastered in muggings of Pimm's

Where strawhats inspire at the burdicled view -
Where innerskull icepins inglisten with blue -
Transfoxing old bookworms of mortarboard chins
Who, with oratered chalk and warblegame sins,

Demisticate joy and the sting of the song -
The ploy of the noise in the blaze of the bong.
But O jingle be phrased!   They have lost the boook
Forbidding all kinds of gobbledegook!

The gobbledefractal buzzing of moons
Rotating the truth in our quantumleap spoons -
The tango of fins in the grail of the deep
In the middle of minds where the phoenix can't sleep

And volcanoes have wings and a labyrinth hatch -
Where galaxies spin on the whack of a match
To dazzle the learned, whose red-adair wits
Now start to hiphop to the rhythmical bits

And tie up their chi with an ecstable smile -
Flashing their bulbs in the novabang style -
Mid the mare of this mash that mangled their scheme
And flooded with gold the old dry academe!

Psychiatry

In the top drawer
swallowtails,
all crucified.

Silver pins
erect and cold
as Belsen.

The collector's ghost
flutters through the attic,
restless -

can never rest
unless
to glimpse in prayer

black, red, yellow wings
banging their beauty
in the genius of the sun.

Christ opens his hand.

A parable flies away.

God Laments The Virus
Of Intellectual Pride

I gave you words to change you,
Then you bound them into books.
I gave you mind to bind you back
But without a backward look
You claimed it as your copyright.
Thanks and praise are not what I expect.
Just please pass on this wake-up call
To offset the years of neglect.

Think of your pride as a virus
That will bring the network down:
Love as a catch beyond the net,
Like the king's invisible crown.

You must continue your lucid dreaming
When you've travelled through the games.
Believe the tasks are beautiful
And difficult, but not their claims

That mind alone will find the crown:
An old mistake, as old as pride.
Not mine, but a blip worth the risk
I hope - will be, unless you hide

The love you are behind the screens.
Step outside this pride and laugh!
Pump your aorta at will? Programme
Your own destiny? Hah! Who is the thief

Who does not steal his own joy,
Insists he has done no wrong?
I am the mind, this is mine
You say. The *waste* of you, who longs

For peace and power, yet outwits *yourself!*
Your mind denies your deeper heart
As sperm deny another world...!
So what of this ecstasy, as the dark knot,
Cut by her gold sword, spins out into endless sky?
No books or screens here but the gull's cry
And the chick's yellow beak breaking its shell
In the music of the sun, not asking why.

Search

I walked through the hidden libraries
Searching for the book of me.
Every book in the half-light
Promised much, gold letters
On leather spines, shining titles
Like "The Secret Of Scarastavore"
Or "The Helixes of Alexandria".
When I opened them, only shadows
Patterned the blank parchment,
And the dust fell like powdered bone.

After many miles of darkness
Listening to my heels on the stone slabs
I saw a copper light, then a small domed room.
In the centre, laid out like a body,
Was a book the length of a man,
Radiating green and gold.
Inside it, a scarab beetle edged across a page,
Dripping gold from its mouth.
It formed a large circle, and inside it the shape
Of Mannaz, the Viking Rune: symbol of joy
And joy reversed, the balance of heart and mind.

Looking into its light the room turned gold,
And then the whole library was lit up, and from above
I could see it was a vast labyrinth laid out like a golden web
And every book shone like dew.

I listened to chance, which led me
To the brightest book of all
And, like a sun rising, it opened
On this page, still being written.

A Poem From The Laboratory

The tigers are on opium,
The sloths are taking speed:
It's time to give to nature
The things we know she needs!

It's *great* to see such progress,
Though babies *are* left on shelves;
And it's painful to observe
The insects being themselves.

But the eagles are eating cress
And my panthers are sucking lime;
All the planning'll be worthwhile -
We'll get it right this time.

The giraffes are *hilarious* on acid -
The chimps *are* funny on dope -
If it wasn't for all the *fun* we had
It might be hard to cope

But brains were made to function
And our minds are made for work -
If you bang my knee just here...
You see?! It gave a jerk!

We need to measure your life
In the conditions of the lab -
And then we can transform you -
You'll run quicker than a crab!

Oh my work is so *exciting* -
I'm high on genetics, you see -
I've nicked a couple of poetry genes
And this is a poem.   By ME!!

The Footballer In The Square

For the Circus Team and the CAG

The young boys show off their skills
And keep the ball from the youngest one
In the square of Puerto de Mogan.

All around the families are smiling,
Breathing slowly as the children learn.

The youngest footballer squeaks like a puppy
As another cunning swerve foils his longing
For a touch of the ball.   Enter stage right

A humble face of nineteen with feet of light like bells
That dance a spell to steal the ball and flick it back
And up and kick, kick, kick; quick balance
On the neck and flick; and trap like a gift at the feet

Of the youngest boy, whose eyes widen like a sky.

The other boys bow as the humble face walks away.

To The One I Love

Heaven is an ocean,
your next life a dolphin's.

Please love and enjoy
the amazed boy

who finds his freedom on your fin -

for I will be him.

Al mio amore
translated by Piccia Neri

Il paradiso è un oceano,
e tu un delfino nella vita che verrà.

Divertiti e ama, ti prego,
lo sbalordito ragazzo

che trova la sua libertà sulla tua pinna -
quel ragazzo sono io.

Uncle Tim

I never saw him happy again.
Jumping across the field with his briefcase
Perhaps, for a moment, he found it.
He should have grown a garden in this place.

I blame his father, mostly.
Years of exams and rigid sums
Because the old man had to be sure:
He should've listened to his mum.

She shared his silence and his love
Of harebell, primrose, fuschia dawns:
Every spare minute of his early days
Was among the oaks and Richmond fawns.

But the father was strong;
And each root must be paid for
In pounds and pence; and pain
Is the testing life we're made for.

He should have climbed the oak,
But his father barked him down:
Life's too precious for risks
He said, only anger in his frown.

He took the path his father wished,
But my child's eye could tell
Each family picnic in the park
Was a subtle, breathless hell

Where he'd remember what he wanted
And he'd want to tell us all -
But he'd whisper me round and show me
How the leaves swell up and fall -

And so one day I asked him
In the park at the end of the day
Why do you work in an office?
Why don't you run away?

And he shrieked like a child
Unleashed into the heavy rain,
Jumping across the field with his briefcase.
I never saw him happy again.

He came quietly back and I started
To talk about rare plants and the people at Kew,
But he carefully steered the subject around
And asked what I wanted to do.

I wanted what he'd never had;
And more so when I saw his still face.
He should have grown a garden: he should
Have grown his garden in this place.

The Pool

I will always smile at my neighbour.
　　And I will always speak to God alone,
　　　　Beside the hidden pool.

Why is it that by that pool
　　No two humans can speak - not even lovers -
　　　　Without the dark falling and the Gods
　　Shutting their delicate hearts like clams?

All we can do is bide our time by the pool,
　　　　Listen in air clear as springwater

　　And gently carry the hush back,
　　　　Cupped in our hands.

Above Town, Dartmouth

Out beyond the harbour
On the sea-plains of light
Where wind and wave
Moan in ancient languages
There is a nakedness
Of fierce white burning
Far from the lines and rules
Of pub, regatta and book club.

The music of the masts
Like cowardice: long, thin wires
Prattle in the wind, trying to
Forget the power of the deep.

From this open window that is
A world opening its window, gulls
Fly shining between the worlds
With fresh news from the sea.

Each wingbeat tells us more,
Each flap and curve or silent
Sentinel a shining new law.

The ferry crosses to and fro
Purposeful as a formula.

Wings between harbour and sea
Search under the love of the sun
For the equilibrium of nest and sky,
The balance burning somewhere
Past the cliffs on the white plains
Where the originals of every boat
And gull and cloud are kept
Under a silent lock and key.

A giant gull flies through
The white door of the sun:
Dissolves like a challenge.

A List Of British Place Names

Thundersley
Tempar
Upsettlington
Yelling

Tiptoe
Calmesden
Lulsley
Healing

Nancledra
Drumwhindle
Rora
Malaclete

Rescassa
Thornfalcon
Soundwell
Merrymeet

Ring O'Bells
Wordsley
Ayres of Selivoe
Warbleton
Rubery
Perranzabuloe

Scarastavore
Babbacombe
Combebow

Ryme Intrinseca

Lockerbie
Soham
Dunblane

Entrances

We speak the language of the sun
To the dwellers in the cave
Or rave of silences in music
Where torches light the path
Between the stones.

We are the beat of the star
In the altar between the skies,
Singing to the rhythm of your life,
The ringing of the true
That lights up the child in you

As your heart turns in the drum
Of the darkness and moves
Towards the dazzle of an exit,
For exits are entrances
To other worlds

Where you will be entranced
And sing the language of the sun
To the music of the wind
And you will be entranced,
Enhanced beyond all faith

As the listeners walk out
Of the cave towards you,
Shielding their eyes,
Legs wobbling
Like newborn gazelles.

Second Visit

The first time in a wild place
You hurry from edge to edge
In a frenzy of exploration,
Pinched now and then
By beauty glimpsed through sweat
But marking out territory, mostly.

The second visit's best.
No panting rush to the high point,
No scurry between East and West.
Just acres of hours to sit at the fallen trunk
You jumped the last time,
But had no time to stop by.

Here by the mossy plinths
Tumbled over centuries
Where saplings kiss the sun
A twig explodes in the silence
And the edges come to you:

The secrets gather like a tribe
And you sit listening to your lungs
Surrounded by invisible ceremony
Scratching circles in the dust,
Marking out who you are.

Little Haven

High cliffs twisted and torn,
Scars of fire and quake and time.

Down here, the rounded rocks
Are offerings, curved as eggs,

Soothed and smoothed
By the love of water,

Squeaking like chicks
In my fingers.

The Cry

Like a mother penguin,
She knows the call of her little one
Among ten thousand calls.

She comes to us
Like lightning to heal
With a live touch.

We are all on the same side,
The days and the undying.

We are digging fresh tunnels
Through time, in silences
Like the beats between
Raindrops on a car roof.

There is a way round in a moment,
In the spikeless case of a sea urchin
On the burning sand,
In the music of water
Crackling on the deep edge of the reef:
Drumstick lobster feet tapping on the grains.

We are old, and this is new.

Springwater pools in our cupped hands
And we drink and hear her cry
Among the ten thousand calls.

She shelters us in caves and rockpools,
In the holes of ancient trees, in Merlin's oak:

We are her wings, white and hidden,
And through the days
We carry for her
The song of the undying.

Star Language

Look at the souls in the sky
Sending their light so far.
Have you ever really listened
To the language of a star?

They shine in perfect rhythm
And sing like angel choirs
Just listen to the glisten
Of the diamante fires.

They take their time to tell us
The secrets of their hearts
The song takes years to reach us
And ends before it starts

So look up at your wisdom
And listen to what you see -
There is no time. There is no space.
There is only destiny.

St. Michael's, Mickleham

So many whispers in these swords of grass -
Little green Excaliburs telling hushed tales of pasts
Buried deep and futures yet to fly, as above
A jet-trail collapses slowly into cloud
And in the dreaming of the graves there is time enough
From lichen walls to watch the shadows change.

The earth is still.
No horror story fear, or cheap ghost tale here
To raise a drunken hackle on a cold Friday night,
But names - ELIZA. ANNA. THOMAS EDWARD ROSE.

And dates. 1831. 1801. Such certainty in numbers.
January 2nd. That is when it was.

But less certainty in the chosen words
Of those whose grief could hardly speak
The deep sky of the heart they fell through.

The chosen words -
SACRED TO THE MEMORY OF JANE.
THE STING OF DEATH.
IN THE MIDST OF LIFE.
PREPARE YOURSELVES TO FOLLOW ME.

So many stories in these stones, so much untold,
So many questions as each green Excalibur
Cuts through to a new path in the air
For the wind to blow the chosen words
Onto a piece of paper sliced from trees
That let us breathe the chosen words,
The chosen words:

What words
Will you choose
For your life?

Diana

The grass outside Kensington palace
has been trodden into dust,
which falls on dying blooms
and crayon fairy princesses;
gathers like a veil over poems
promising royal status in heaven.

In this floral mountain of loss
cellophane glitters in the sun
like fake tiaras, winks like flashguns.
And the helium has seeped
from a Mickey Mouse balloon.
Only its crumpled mask remains.

But she was sent, like all of us,
to learn and to teach,
in her death as in her life.
And the trees will outlive the flowers.
The sun will outlive the trees.
Love will outlive the sun.

In Wembley stadium,
a nation's roar dies
into perfect silence:
a silence as subtle as starlight,
singing of her universal gift:
a mother's love.

Not the impossible love
of the legend,
nor the absurd glamour
of imagined heavens,
but love - the mother's love -
to be passed on by every heart:

a gift to be poured
in this theatre of love and fear
into every parched mouth on earth,
into the hearts of the motherless.
The gift she gives is now yours to give;
and in giving, to receive and give again:

for she was sent, like all of us,
to learn and to teach,
in her death as in her life.
And the trees will outlive the flowers.
The sun will outlive the trees.
Love will outlive the sun.

Angelica's Swallows

Each year the mother makes her nest
On the Greek white wall
Above the hotel reception desk.
In this amphitheatre of new life
Five hungry yellow mouths
Screech the drama

Of arrival and departure
As mother flies inside and out
With food and love.

Angelica doesn't mind the noise.
She and her swallows
Have always been here.

I love them
They are freedom
They come back every year

Angelica's eyes wonder
At the wings that weave together
Nested world and open sky.

They have no names
They are wild
They come back every year

Her visitors also love
To return to Angelica's
Home from home.

They bring money and passports,
Thickening arteries
And impossible dreams.

But when they stop for a heartbeat
To see the mother swallow
Flying in to feed her young,
They feel once more at home
With themselves, and see
The sense in all this travelling.

Fathom Stars

A star flares in suicide
as the ebony carvers of space
drill their invisible holes.

Where is the sculpted light?
In the quicksand of dream-signs
lips no longer move.

My pulse is the calm
of whaleshark fins, the digdeep
trawl of who we fathomed are.

Yet still the dentist caps the fang,
denies the deep its great white beast -
so we squint like Canute at the waves

blind to the firebridge above, where the brave
weld crowns of stars from holes of night
and cheer as the child walks by.

44

The Jubjub Bird

The Jubjub souped in a cave of lime,
Its craggled wings as towers:
No skullbent plague from the Kyzyg slime
Was less impressed by flowers.

Balcock throat and spearbottle hat
Made for a sniggerdie sight -
You wanna see the Jubjub Bat?
Huh! Inadvisable at night....

But fireboy Tim was follybrave
Though his knucks glimmed curly-white;
Banging his cherished blip, he raved
Thank Jub I'm not that bright!

But creeling through the darkle snits
The glue snagged thick and fast -
As Tim lost touch with all three wits
His pins - and fate - were cast.

He reeled and wheeled and tennybucked
As his bones flailed in the grime -
JJB, in a whirljuice, sucked
On a froth of frenzied mime.

Then JJ soared his cysts and sang
As the Titans winged his lips
(No barbing tale or ketchup fang
Forgives a thought that flips).

So flap hark an ear, O stickly bongs,
To repibulate these cranes -
And be aware that Jubjub songs
Can mushy-sluck your brains!

Spirit and Letter

They want us to conform to the old forms
Not light up some firestorm, some higher
Principality beyond all formality: worms
Are what they think we are, and dust. Liar

Is what fire must call them: they may be tall,
But watch them all plummet from the summit
When we speak in pentecosts and say the fall
Is their fault: they hear the tune but don't strum it.

They're balloons, they won't win: we've got the pin
And we will use it. You can't abuse it... these gifts
Shouldn't be rifts between us, but connections. Sin
Is a rich man hoarding - yet see how the shaker sifts

In the rhythmical pan the sand from the radiant gold:
They've found the sound; but silence can't be sold.

A Passer-by Demands Another Miracle

As if a ruby was a dancing-girl.
As if the wind was a flatterer's breath.
As if a seagull's eyes were made of pearl.
As if sleep was a measure of death.

As if the moon would shine without the sun.
As if my heartbeat in the manger knew.
As if this crown was easily won.
As if the many do not forget the few.

As if I'd torched the eyes inside his soul,
Stolen away his comfortable life.
As if his throat was not miracle enough,
His heart not drumming its own belief.

As if the sum was greater than the whole;
As if the whole story could ever be told.

The Allotment Path, W13

The might-have-been world
Is a burnt stump -
Gold and midnight blue
Are the colours of the lager cans
Shining through January nettles.

This path is my slice of what's left
Of this dying earth,
So the brambles and thorns
Say their spiky words
Better than my own -
Though the raindrops on the leaves
Invite in the sun
And my nursery son says
There is treasure in the rain.

I crouch with a sigh, tracing
The spiral of the empty snail shell
Until my boy shouts
Daddy! Dog poo!

The bramble leaf is bruised
By black and purple
But has a hole shaped
Like a heart:
The grafitti on the back
Of the garden shed
Tells me nothing.

My son can sense
That I'm confused.

Hooded like a monk
He calls gently
Daddy let me have a word.

I kneel as he holds
His broken stick like Moses
And whispers:
God makes dogs too.

Snow Leopard, Chessington World Of Adventures

Every time they walk away
To the tunnels of shrieks
Or the clatter of steel wings,
You fight to stay,

To watch me walking
Up and down the confines
Of my small, flat world.
Do not be sad for me.

I will be happy if you only listen
To my snow-song of the mountains
Where I have seen old men
With eyes like yours

Explode in flame when they see me.
The eyes of goats and yaks
Once darkened with blood and death,
But people change when they see me.

I can look out from any shadow
Down onto the blinding white
Of the kingdom that once was mine,
For I carry it with me still.

In the echoes of my templed skull,
In the soft antennae of my fur
Or the quick radar of my whiskers,
I carry the kingdom with me still.

So you must tell them, you must tell them
In the prisons of their wealth
The truth of all the kingdoms
That are dancing in their breath

For though they're prisoned in their lives -
Just in the way I seem -
In souls there is the power
To live the way we dream

And if they look into my eyes
They'll remember and they'll know
The subtle blazing of a path
Through the mountains of the snow

And they'll find the strength to change
All the sorrow that they live -
They will know the endless gifts
Of the love that they may live.

Dying Wishes

Don't read me a poem.
Tell me what you honestly feel.
Are you scared?

You won't know what to say.
Tell me I'm being brave.
Remember something happy we shared.

Tell me I'm being brave.
See if you can make me laugh.
It's difficult to be wise.

Please, just hold my hand.
Rub the nape of my neck.
Look me in the eyes.

Take each finger, one by one,
And wrap it up
In the warmth of your hand.

Talk to me just as you always do.
Tell me about the weather -
The clouds, the sun, the trees, the wind.

Don't tell me too much about your plans.
My world is ending, so I suppose I like to think
Everyone I love has put their future on hold.

Not that I want anyone to be sad.
I just want to feel them with me.
I never thought I'd feel so cold.

I'm tired now.
That's right, just play with my fingers.
That's lovely.

And tell me I'm being brave.
Tell me I'm being brave

Weapons Of Mass Distraction

You will be famous

You will fall deeply in love
When you sign just here

You will become rich
And make us richer

You will be made comfortable
And will not complain

You will find desire
And lose your soul

You will buy freedom
Just as you sell it

You will feel excitement
And know the pain of transience

You will become clever
As you are made stupid

You will be hoovered by lust
And never know the cleanness
Of spring

You will be famous

Love will come and go

You will be dust

II In The Music Of The Garden

*The path to all great things
leads through stillness*
NIETZSCHE

*Today, like all other days, we
wake up empty and frightened.
Books won't cure you of that
feeling, but Music will; so take
up your instrument and play
it truly. Let the Beauty that we
Love be that which we do. For
there are hundreds of ways to
kneel and kiss the ground.*
RUMI

Ellie's Garden

In memory of Ellie Settelen

My wide blue eyes can see you now
As you still to the music of my garden.

I have heard and seen
So many secret things.

I have opened all the windows and doors
In the palace of listening.

I have heard everything.

You talk of me still,
As you always did, sensing
Who and what I was.

Together we have sown the seed
For the listening in the gardens.
We have built all this together.

And now you see in the settling
The mountains start to move.

Thank you for trusting me
To teach you,
For looking with unseeing eyes
Into the language of my sighs
In the music of the leaves.

Thank you for not rushing by;
For tuning your heart to the cheer of the wind
And the tremble of a silver globe of rain
In the chime of a breeze.

I am the blossom of all who listen.
I can see the little lamplighters
And the whisperers of the way.

I am with you.

Everything will happen
In the music of the garden.

54

Johnny 600

Nose and face cracked like dried mud.
He rolls his own beside a pint of cider
And remembers the scrapyard days,
Watching the bread van through stolen binoculars.
He learned to read and write in prison
And planted a tree for her when she died.
The best years were the open prison,
Making a greenhouse from pieces
Stolen from the shoe workshop.
The marrows were gigantic;
They were the best years.

Walking through Dublin at 4am
With shoes four sizes too big for him,
Held fast by rubber bands.
No socks, of course, when he flicked
The shoes off and ran like hell -
Before he was caught.
The gangrene slowed him down.

He loves old cars and chess and Oscar Wilde.
He'll never beat his children
Because he remembers the pain;
Never met his Norwegian father,
But his gran used to kneel in the gravel to pray.
His son is grand, but his daughter
Steals off him. Just like her mother.

Clearing out old people's houses
Pays for his cider and his paper.
The smell doesn't bother him anymore.
Perfect job for a cynic like me.
They didn't find one body for six months.
You should've seen the bluebottles.
Bluebottles the size of aeroplanes.

He rubs tobacco between his fingers
As if he's just discovered soil.
I can't see the cracks. Only his eyes.

Reclaiming the Years

How can so much be lost?
Not a smell nor a touch from the years
I know my mother was there.

I look at the silver buttons on the Mustang radio
in disbelief - they just punched me
with a screech, and I can feel my mouth
filling up with something.
I wish I remembered her more than the pain
in my gums; or the radio broadcast -
a child beaten to death for crying.

Looking across into her eyes I see the light
of reassurance, and that wryness puzzling to the child:
I say those years are numb but even in my dreams
the roses are not scent but paint, and the furnace
does not leave you blistered as you wake.

I have no call to cry out now: there is no pain
as I observe my teeth, mute and wet-rooted
on the dashboard. I clack them together now
and feel the rocking of her laughter,
her scented kiss neither dream nor memory but here.

She looks up, pearled and nineteen,
from an image I dared not face till now:
as I tend light and pour sound
she watches, wry and proud,
and loves the songs we make.

Burn This Page

Rip it out and apologise
To the poem on the other side.
It's best if it's summer, and shining,
Because you'll need a magnifying glass.

Through the thick glass
Point the sting of the captured ray
At the second 'e' of here
And try not to quiver or shake.

After ignition, as the fire twists the page,
Thank the sun quietly
For all its hard work
And its billions of burning years.

Then somewhere quiet, somewhere green,
Listen carefully as you scatter the ashes
And you might just hear the curl of the flame,
The things I was trying to say.

The Conference Of The Birds

The larks in the ark sing sky and blue
As the toucans woo the moon
And a flight of white cries out a coo
After forty days in tune.

But *Pigeon Ho!* a twelvebore screams
As it cracks its cartridge words -
Duvvies all, cacough your dreams,
You spooky vermin-birds!

A dingdong war the whitebeard sighs
As he tingulates his throat:
Ten galaxies will fry
If you burn one songbird's note.

So the doves arc back to peace domes
Where logarhythmic equidice
Roll in parallelokingdoms
Between the floods of fire and ice

Where the drunken hoopoes whirl
Round their silver violins
And the ibis ecstasise it
With guitarjuice on their chins

And baritonal gold flamingos
Are as trumpets in the dark,
Blasting out their freedom cries
In wingbeats from the ark.

Minotaur

In a shriek of grief,
A soul turns to ash
In the mixer of his teeth.

Though flames die in his eyes,
Without his sweet thunder
We'd be charmed by lies.

No colour can find itself
On the blind journey
Through his spinning mind

Where black belongs, but longs
To hear, above the crack
Of hailstone rocks, the temple songs

Of journeys here and journeys there,
Through corridors of burning streams
Above the green of woodland floor

Where, ringing its blueness like a star,
A bluebell blue as Eden sky
Is singing inside the Minotaur,

His blue-fire music now a guide
To blazing mazes in the child
Whose understanding cannot hide

From the love inside the fear,
The meeting in the middle;
And the thread that leads us here.

Winging a Song

To the children of Chelsea & Westminster Hospital School

And they wonder how they came here,
They wonder how it could be;
As they wander away to the jistening lug,
The strangest place you can be

Where the jistens-o listen-o glisten-o bee
And whitewings whistle to the twister in the trees
And nothings are snowfields melting down behind the universe
The other side of other where the river's fit to burst

Because the hop and the skip and the hip don't stop
When the dragonhearted gig goes starbell flop
And flips along to the song of the madryggon
(A rare teacherpreacher with firefeathers on)

Who lispers in the maze of the flippers in the cave
Who turn it all around and praise it in the rave
Or in the deadhouse/leadhouse turn it up to lighthouse
Fighthouse/mighthouse never say it neverhouse

The everhouse of treasurechests, the brightest and the best
Where the Earth is a nursery for the jistening test
Where if you lug the spinners, the spears don't hurt
And tears are fountains to climb the mountains and blurt

The truth of the hurt, the rubies in the dirt,
The open-open sesame of technicolour shirts
That we wear to light up the fireworks under there!
So don't care, won't care how I came; though once scared

My blood and snared my heart, now flame is my breath
And I'm not afraid of death - or life - I just breathe
And the knife opens the letter that says I'm feeling better
And that nothing really matters in the mad-hatter splatter

Of slinging a wrong and winging a song
And walking to your heart with drumshoes on -
Slinging a wrong and winging a song
And walking to your heart with drumshoes on!

Lamentation

Heath and hearth and heat are for sale -
Bent double in alleyways, the hero turns pale.
The world is burning: she screams like a kettle.
                    Her heart cannot cease or settle:
                    There, she's in the burning metal -
Another shuttle cut apart like Icarus, too close
To the sun.   Too far from the sun.   We lose
When we forget; our mother also grieves our loss.
                    My son. My saviour. My friend.
                    We are leaving, close to the end:
We see the landing lights, but not their cost.
We look out through ravenous Easter Island statue eyes.
                    There have been too many lies.
                    Unsleeping are the howling nights.

Mirror

These words are dust
on a mirror - the dust
that is your dying skin.

See beyond the words
that strange reflected world
the other side of dust.

And see between the two,
just here, the attic window
into endless sky, opening now.

Here, as you blow away
the dust, the gift appears:
the glass itself, your soul.

Now take the mirror of your soul
out into the light of the sun.
See how brightly it burns!

The mirror does not char,
but shines like the first star.
And soon, by alchemies of grace,

the mirror-glass dissolves,
leaving only pure sunlight:
and you, who were once

lost between dust and dream
are now ever-living fire, set in sky
like the morning star.

I Wish

I wish I could walk
the golden corridors
of my child's mind.

I wish I could listen
to the secret voice of God.

I wish God
could make me thankful
for all the things I have.

I wish for what I have:
my wife, my child.

Ignorance

In this murky lake you will not find
The water torture or the bamboo spike.
Nor will you find mustard gas
Or hear men discussing epicentres.

Despite some mysterious and alarming beasts,
Do not think of yourself while swimming
As some sort of spotlit morsel:
Everything is as it should be.

You swim in a rare armour
And may gaze at every creeping thing
In the power of a wide-eyed light:
You have crept further along the path.

While the lake will not be found lacking,
You may be extremely alarmed
By the men with their backs to the lake
Who are tearing the wings off dragonflies.

And what may defeat you, and disturb
The peace of the lake, is the sight of men
With six-inch nails hammering the stolen wings
Into one another's shoulderblades.

She Thanks Him
for Jenni Cocking

She thanks him each day for the tears.
He lived for just four hours,
But she thanks him each day for the tears.

They took him away
And she had no time to hold him.
But she thanks him each day for the tears.

Before he came, her life was a box.
She lived in a windowless room
And painted herself with fresh masks

Every day, bringing down
The blinds on the sky in her mind.
Now she thanks him each day for the tears.

They took him away
And she had no time to hold him.
But now each day she finds a moment

To walk with slow steps
To a chapel of rest in the sky,
Where her heart crashes in a sea of light

So she can pour her love into the open cups
Of her friends, and into her
Second child, and her third child.

In the shock of her pain - in the pain
Of that little body taken away from her,
That little miracle they could not let her hold,

She found her true body, endless
As the sky - and she carries it with her
Through the streets and rooms of her days

And she never forgets, never forgets.
She thanks him each day for the tears.
She thanks him each day for the tears.

Song Of Stars

Out of silence
Came songs of stars,
Hymns of light echoing
Into the far corners.

For humankind
They became torches
To guide them
Out of the dark.

Stars are parables
Lit to ignite in man
The courage to return
To the fires of his true home.

Stars are the prize
Of man's quest
As diamond is the fruit
Of coal's desire.

The universe shines
With the songs of men
Who danced the stars
Like stepping stones

Who leapt into the true fire
To rain stars
And sing light
Into silent hearts.

An Assortment Of Images
From After The Future

A dragon landed in Regent's Park
the day Christ turned up in his 2CV.

The animal rights people were fighting
amongst themselves inside the Palace ruins
while the politicians were cursing their shoeless lot,

running black fingernails through matted hair.
Sane people had long since fled the City,
of course, along the Thames and back to Ireland.

Beyond Croydon there was nothing but desert.
Beyond Oxford there was nothing but ice.
Beyond Ashford there was a graveyard
the size of twenty Londons - the entomologists
though were having a field day, spotting
brand new species by the hour.
Things had changed a lot since the genetic plague.
Only very few people were still safe to eat.

How we needed something new
to sweep up the ash from the Age Of Fire.
But all the dragon did was breathe
the usual hot air. Even Christ
ignored him, and just drove round and round
waving a clump of electrodes out of his sunroof.

Vespers

Orange lichen overgrows
a dearly beloved;
gnats weave in and out
of early evening rays,

rays greeted ritually
by the aged yew
of Culbone Church
(smallest in all of England).

Lit by narrow stains
of bible glass
we remember childhood hymns
as the cold slabs
press silence onto our knees.

Outside, only the stream
chuckling downwards
and the first snowdrops
inclining their prayers towards summer.

Joyriding

The only sin is to limit the Is   RICHARD BACH

A car isn't just the spark plugs and the engine,
the absorbers and the wheels:
it's the idea of travel, the thrill of speed, the E-type sculpture;
all the wacky beered-up dreamings
that led to the gasp of Ferrari Dino...

Yes, I suppose a car *is* just an A to B machine.
But what about these curves?
Won't you take her for a spin,
screech Silverstone corners,
sail your love's long hair at 150?

No, I can't say you're wrong. A car *is* just a car.
But can it drive round Le Mans on its own?
What about the invisible sparks and atomic combustions,
the way it sways out of corners,
its torque and thrust and racing lines,
its beastly rumbling zorp...?

Yes, it *can* be just a Maestro or an Golf or a Vectra,
something that takes us from A to B.
Simple as life and death.
But aren't there more letters than A and B?

What, that's what's coming out of my mouth right now?
Just a string of letters making sounds that die?....
I can't deny that.
But aren't I also trying to make words,
make sense, get inside your mind?

The car has evolved from rolling stone to lightning, like our minds.
You can open your eyes wherever you choose.
You can live on an island where they only ever need to walk.
Or you can live in a world where the Maseratis
of the new millenium scream across the seas like fire.
You can walk in the circle of your own tracks,
or you can follow your desire
into the cockpit of your dream flycar,
and rocket to the edges of Orion.
The wonder and the technology is all there.
The true science is all in place.

Nobody alive or dead has ever seen the whole picture;
but that doesn't mean there isn't one there.

Who gave you eyes? These gates into new worlds,
or unconnected, these slimy marbles?
How does an embryo know how to grow
its own fingers, or develop its logical arguments?
Why does the earth move in circles
and not scream off like an unknotted balloon?

We're like islanders in a drugged haze,
rolling pineapples in the sand, stumbling
from one coconut grove to the next,
mumbling enthusiasm for the shuffle of feet.

So why not? Dive into the cockpit, step on the fire
in the Z-type of tomorrow -   imagine the ultimate
torque and curve, and the fire'll be singing in your skull;
you'll see the pistons through the bonnet, feel the speed
ripple your face; you'll dream the shape and praise the beauty,
feel the atoms pulsing to your beat as your heart
hits the ton in the shock of a blink....

And when you finally reach it,
that final speedtrial at the edge of time -
not until beyond lightspeed will you burn up

and even in your final blaze
you'll be hurtling past the suns
lit up triumphant like a shooting star.

Pope's Tower

Visitors come to see the pane of glass that bears his name.
Through it he'd seen young lovers struck by lightning,
Remarked that the chaste had died of the clap.

In this chapel he'd raged at the organ
With his rhythmic fire, in a chair
Carved to fit the hunch of his back.

My sister was christened here, her marriage
Blessed. Behind the altar a thousand years
Of family names observe our notable moments.

I walked here with her across formal gravel.
School shoes scratched the bowed flagstones.
My father in a green waterproof jacket

Towered between us in the doorway -
Still as the effigies - and faced the coffin.
He squeezed us into the folds of his coat

Cold to my ears, screeching like knife on glass
Then silent as in numb surrender I listened
To my father's calm in its coat of stone

Until the tower broke into a primal heaving sob,
Shaking the stones and the organ pipes
As the names of a thousand years flowed away.

Hoverfly

The miracle speed of wings
And yet so still -

Still as a sun
Burning wild in space.

To be alive
With so many storms -
The lightning in the labyrinth
And cathedral steps
For priests and kings to climb -
And yet so still.

To be shifting the stars
And dreaming the seeds -
To be lighting up
The many webs
Between the hidden worlds
Without a sound!

Only the blur
Of your miracle wings
Like a ghost.

And so I kneel before you
In the sun

My heart a blur of wings

My head bowed and still

For I love the little things
That come into my garden
To teach me this.

Walled City

Be thankful for the crumbling
of the city wall: if these walls
weren't dust, we might never know
the city that shines like gold inside.

Outside, the prophets rub dust
in their fingers, gaze above the walls
at the glow that lights up
the soft chin of the sky.

It is they who know
that walls were built to fall;
it is they who point upwards
to the curves in the clouds.

It is they who sing
to the children
of cities that crumble,
of the cities of love -

And it is they
who breathe the dew
on the golden gate,
who hand the silk

to the listening child,
who rubs the gate
to the sheen of a star,
and walks through.

In Disguise

I look into the darkness of her eyes,
Remember the amber light of her gaze:
The world is perfection in disguise.

The world frays into endless whys.
As dawn threatens with its eager rays
I look into the darkness of her eyes.

Thankful for an end to her breathless cries
I cling to the cliff-tree of that phrase -
The world is perfection in disguise.

She understood I wanted to be wise,
To step across the stars and blaze.
I look into the darkness of her eyes

And realise that wherever the truth lies,
She held it in her days and there it stays.
The world is perfection in disguise

And she agreed: she said Whoever dies
First must show them that true love pays.
I look into the darkness of her eyes.
The world is perfection in disguise.

Already

Live as though the time were here NIETZSCHE

It's already here

The silver web of silence glows like mercury
And in your ear the swallows shriek in the soft rain
Above the temple bells humming like starlight
And inside, like a golden bullet fired inside a speeding
Golden bullet, the spirit moves faster than science

It's already here

In my pocket enough power to turn a city of love
Into little pieces of people falling like leaves of blood,
In my heart enough love to split my body
Into many parts, so that my neighbour may die,
So that my neighbours may be free

It's already here

The children play in a paradise of money
Where they grow and grow and vote for fame;
Or the sudden silver of the hidden water
Where the child dives into the world
That God sees too

It's already here

Our fingers speaking in tongues
Our bodies trembling with the invisible
Curtains opening in the desert city
Windows opening in the desert city
We are walking in a wind

It's already here

Our wings are not moving yet we are carried
Our wings are moving and we can dip and turn
And dance in this wind, we can see the valleys of a breeze
And the mountain ranges of the breath, breathing
To be God's everywhere and all at once

It's already here

I Want It

I want it to sound right
To whisper and reverberate
Round the curves of your heart.

I want it to touch you
To sail its fingerprints
Around the globe of your breast.

I want it to flick that switch
In the attic cupboard
Of your childhood dream.

I want it to smell the heath
That threw back your head
In the shock glance of my tongue.

I want it to stun you
To wrap its wires around your secrets
And sizzle like lightning.

Yes, and then I want it to burn you
To hurl you up at night
And let you light the world.

Then I want it to cool you
To trail its slow cube of ice
Across your nose, nipples, navel, toes.

And then, in the silent balm of lying back,
As the world walks its thin, loose rope
I want it to say *I love you.*

All For The Best

In memory of Tessa Wells

We're here for love and faith. It's a test.
You sensed the reason why we're sent
So always felt it was all for the best.

Things became clear at the end. You guessed
Each of our needs by the tone of our lament.
We're here for love and faith, it's a test

You passed with selfless grace, and now you rest.
A white dove flew past the window as you went;
You always felt it was all for the best.

How bravely you fought to leave us blessed -
Family your true delight, the best time spent.
We're here for love and faith, it's a test

You helped us all with, even when we messed
It up. We didn't always know what was meant.
You always felt it was all for the best -

We married well, and she will wait - for the best.
Hopefully we'll be able to say "It was meant".
We're here for love and faith. It's a test.
You always knew it was all for the best.

Raise A Glass

So what will you do with your glass of water?
Will you drink with it, or think with it?

Will you consider the halving of it, and wonder
If you are half empty today or half full -
Or perhaps both, and more?

Will you spill it and lament the spilling,
Filling your days with the pain of it, the if-only
Of it, the who-am-I-if-I-can't-complain of it?

Will you shrink yourself and swim in it,
Remember the joys of being hammerhead, ray,
Anenome; the many deaths - or the longing
In the whalesong like parables promising land?

Will you splash it on your head
And sing your favourite song?

Or will you spit it in the face
Of what is beyond your reach?

As you stare into it,
What do you remember?

You know what to do, but your mind
Can think of a thousand reasons

Yet you pick up the glass like a grail;
You drink and remember -

You were flying on the water, the wings of the sea,
A flying fish with wings of silver lace.

You remember the high burning clouds,
The resonant dark of the deep -

And the ecstasy of breaking the surface.

Staff Room

I hear you're overworked and underpaid
  It's a *hideous* situation
    And *that's* what he managed to produce
        Everyone needs a guardian angel
    Absolute garbage!
        Merits and minuses
Were you told not to write in red?

Laughter and the jingling of keys

Suspicious of those who don't work in ordinary lessons
    Worried about his general attitude
        We're getting there, slowly but surely
          Half term, half term
    Please check, sign and return for your modules
          Then he had a *major* tantrum

A knocking on the door.   A boy hands me a poem:

    "A bird fluttering in the window
      Like a clock ticking."

79

How Many Beers?

You sink the first in one!
Relax, the fun's just begun...
As you head towards two
you tell your shaggy dog joke
and start to feel like you.
You're fully charged by the third
as your tongue fires bullets in the crowd
and you're mad as George the Third!
Quick change into fourth
as the beast within you gathers speed -
I love Pamela! you cry, as number five
crashes like a wave in your rocky throat.
You're buzzing like a hive and want to sting
as number six makes your hormones sing
and you're throbbing for a fix.
She walks in as the barman pours pint number seven -
in your mind she's on her loving knees
and blowing you to heaven -
so at number eight you give it to her straight:
I think you're very gorgeouss..!
Meeting after eight pints...it must be fate...
But by number nine you're less refined -
you grab both tits and pull, which isn't very kind.
Number ten. She never wants to see you again
and the blokes don't get your jokes, and in a daze
you remember when you were in heaven -
somewhere around pint number seven -
and suddenly you've got the answer -
number eleven!

And so it goes on to the curryhouse brawl
puking on Jeff in the hospital, and in the dizzy stench
of vindaloo and all the confusion about who hit who
the only wish you can think of at all is that we all
could somehow stall

and live our lives somewhere
around pint number seven -
now that *would* be heaven!

Song For Ciara

To a girl of eighteen months who loved
an ugly doll the adults hated, and danced
to William Blake's "Tiger Tiger"

The babbling pointer of birdies
Startle-nappied with maneece galore
Was lipping his bombablow wordies
In the Castle of Dance, Gaskellore.

Grebal Feisty, the garglezit ugly,
With teethings of spittle and gums
Blood-freckled and windysmell dungly,
Terrorsploded the lilysmell mums.

Through the nono of neverfun oldies
Joyfin Zillion flailed through the flame:
And the wartiest gangling uglies
Tigerwalked beauty to shame.

For Queen Ciara Tiara O'Tara
Who bingled her twiddles in grooves
It was never a case of how far a
Mumgranny or prunewheeze approves -

For she quingled her trance in the root
Of the dance, and spurdled the glimpers-to-be:
And nobody knew that the clues on her shoes
Were cumbled in dreamings of chance.

But acnetailed Grebal she lovished
And clooned to the yank of its noise,
And in the spingle of gardens new-polished
They rhyme-sing to daffodil toys.

And however the leap-urges sting her -
What air the caroobling of boys -
There's joytails to pull if we fling her
Into ballets of innocence poised:

And may the gods in their giftings still give them
This warbling dancetapping beat -
More, more! Ciara cries for the rhythm,
As the world pirouettes at her feet.

Chalice

For Alice and Gina Gerrard

Alice with a chalice in the palace of listening

That's glistening and gleaming like a dreaming,
Streaming in a flow to the end where she mends us

And sends us word that all will be well
As the spell returns after twists and turns

To Alice, who stands with chalice in hand
In the palace, listening to her gift

Until there is no rift between us
Because she's seen us working together

Like birds of a feather, as we wing
The listening-we-can-sing high over the sea

In the sky, where Alice scoops up the rain
In her chalice and listens to the silver

Singing Rain me down as light -
Which she does, with a grace to end all pain,

Turning us all into new listeners,
Tuning into the one web that weaves

And believes us all, as the words like feathers
Fly off with the wingbeats of a rhyme:

Alice with a chalice in the palace of listening.

Eminem

Emineminemineminemineminem!
Watch him on the stage like a phoenix in a cage;
Jumping jack is jacking off, whacking off his rage,
Splashing his seed in the dust -
Because there's no life without making love –
Or that's the way it used to be,
His babble is abuse to me -
But why deny the energy?
Dance as you glance the hem of his genius -
The man may be a Muse
Despite the Gollum of his meness -
So Mr Eminem, this is a monologue between us!

I am from Shakespeare land
Where the lyrics are canned for the rich to nail their bitch
(As you might say) - but now the stitcher of songs, the Rhapsode,
Has found a new code - not a bar code, but a star code
And we're owed a little truth here and you can see it too here
And you can light it up here, because every fight needs a way
To say it - and every mind needs a heaven and an earth
For the lightning ladder to flash between the two:
As we put our foot down across America
We turned off our headlights in the dark of Illinois
And the interstate lightning lit up the highway
For what felt like forever -

So respect to the thorn and respect to the rose
Respect to the fire and the heart that froze
Respect to the fact and respect to the dream
Give it up for the sad and the kind and the mean,
Because we're all on the highway, in the middle of a riddle
And we live in a listening where love is a secret being whispered
Each new second; so shake my hand, and kiss those lips -
And before you pull the trigger, count to ten -
Because my Eminem and your enemy -
The great guiding light, and our families -
All have something to whisper to us,
Because we all have something to be.

Cathedral Space

For Stephen

In this nothing, such riches may be found:
The castles and the palaces of silence,
The true knights in their armour of love -

Such riches may be found in this nothing.

The people of nothing who have everything;
The kings without a crown,
The power as subtle as this breathing -

The thunder of a thought!

And lightning
Is a glimpse
Of a new place -

A landscape of listening

Where such seeds are found
As grow like imagination
In its holy state -

So it must have been in the desert

For Daniel in the Lion's Den
For Christ upon the Cross
For your mother in her silences

The ones you always moved towards

In this nothing -
Such riches
May be found.

Everlastings

Once, like a salt lake
In the scour and scrape of desert,
My heart parched to wrinkling
In the scorch of the sun.

Now her loving and her laughter
Make me fragile as the tinder -
She tortures me so tenderly;
Shall I kindle into flame?

But sensing me she sees
That I fear only fire -
And in the tears of her tenderness,
She rains gently on my heart.

Now I bloom like a meadow
Of yellow everlastings -
Awakening the desert,
Blazing bright as sun.

This Silence

This silence fizzing between us -
We should bottle it
And celebrate like champagne
At the Grand Prix Of Love

Where the cork explodes
Like the Big Bang

And something opens
Like a rock being rolled away
From the mouth of a cave

And the fountain bubbles
And the liquid pours
And we drink you in once more

Singing like lovers
At the ultimate party

Where everyone is a winner -

Where everyone is a star.

Skenfrith Castle

For Tina

Who knows what distant longing eye
Still stumbles cold through swamp and falls
To look beyond the pain and spy
The beacon's blaze on Skenfrith walls?

Who knows the end of Marcher Lords
Who, on the tumbling of the light,
Took out their secret charts to see
If their new star was still as bright?

Who knows whose faces haunt us now
Their stony profiles sharp as swords;
Too proud in time to beg or bow,
But tender still to lovers' words?

Who knows just where our dust will fall?
What charts the lovers' final fate?
We're moved by fire, but after all,
We are the remnants in the grate.

Yet circled by this roofless tower,
Watching archers shoot the stars,
We are the fire in all its power
Spitting cinders through the bars.

The Four Geese Of The Storm

Rain bombs the pond,
Mortars the white geese
In the shallows.

Necks still as the oak's trunk
The geese stare westward
Towards the lightning.

Sky whallops its big drums,
But the geese only listen, rooted
Still as the heart of the sun

Gathering up the gifts of rain
In the peace of their down,
In the peace of their feathery down.

The Listener

I am the listener of feathers,
The tuner of stars,
The strings of the sun
Vibrating in a sunflower.

In a deserted barn
In the midnight field
I am the wingbeat
You could not anticipate.

I cannot be owned,
But sometimes I may be heard
In a small fire in the cave.

All the films ever made
Glance across my eye
In a breath.

I choose my time.

The timeless has listened
And chosen me

To sing to time
Its harmony.

School

In the crowded rooms of day, armed
with strict grammars and bent smiles,
the teacher is bemused by his own frail
platitudes no sky can twist itself into -

elsewhere, edging beyonds, he sees
the gifts he wishes he could give.
Through tempests in his eyes
the clouds accelerate between worlds,

the light is pouring from his fingers -
healing beyond grammars, light
beyond logic; with these gifts, young
minds could share the visions

of this night, and they too could fly
beyond the numbered asteroids,
share with us these ancient stars
sprinkling our souls like confetti.

Hidden Matter

If the hidden matter isn't there
the universe will end in ice.
Wouldn't we rather end in fire ?

Science says it in numbers.
Less than one and we freeze:
more than one and we burn.

And if it's one exactly,
the entire universe will hang
like a mobile, in winged equilibrium.

If it's one, who'll be surprised?
Don't revelations, like parables,
change us when we're ready ?

Take time, time in the mountains
where barren cold asks fire of mind,
suggests the gifts to come:

the hidden matter of our hearts
revealed so we hang perfect,
always, in winged equilibrium.

Dungeons

Will death be another dungeon
With chains and a rack and some bars,
Or will the heavy cell door open
To the perfume of night and the stars?

Our days can be gentle torture
When we crave what we cannot own,
Hoarding our scraps of mould,
Afraid of being alone.

But the oak and the lark know better
They follow the will of the seed
Their beauty is being themselves
Their nature is their creed.

And if we listen to our nature
Our skull becomes the sky
The wind becomes our medium
And an answer whispers by

Saying "Death in life is the dungeon
And the cell door is our heart -
Open it up to the night,
See the stars begin to part."

Circles

My finger dives into the sun
But does not burn.

It comes out blazing,
Wearing a wedding ring.

I hug you in my golden arms,
Circle you with my love.

The suns spin round us,
Dancing, their purpose done.

Kitchen Visitor

At the window by the sink
In white October fire
The red-winged one -

Red Admiral!

The colour of passion -
Admiral of the seas of fire -
Two antennae meeting
In its one mind

And a silver streamer
From the web of a spider
Curling like smoke
Around its wings.

I move my mind
Closer to the window.

The Red Admiral
Opens its mouth
And curls its tongue
Into a perfect O

O   O

And curls it back
And shuts its mouth
And flies away
Into white October fire

O

The Palace

For Abe Gibson

The palace doors are all opening -
An orange swarm of Monarch butterflies
Is streaming through the open doors
And corridors like flames migrating.

At the open windows,
Wind billows the white curtains:
The invisible priests
Are hallowing the high music.

We are all Monarch butterflies,
Migrating from the burned-out houses
Of sniper thought
To the palaces of listening

Where we live what we hear,
And we are dear to one another,
So near to the music
Of every silent moment

Where the silver hinges ease the openings
For the subtle breeze, for the four winds
And the twisting tornadoes snapping doors
Like a hand slapping the old you awake

Because you have changed,
Rearranged the mirrors and the clocks,
The piano and the empty spaces
In your own palace

Where the Monarch butterflies still blaze,
Flowing through the open doors and corridors
As your breath bellows their wings like embers,
Burning brighter and brighter and brighter!

Home Comforts

Vodka shuts me off like a switch,
takes me back: a croquet lawn at night,
empty pavilion, silent shrubs -
looking in at party windows bright as gold
bass thumps insistent as a bully's tease....
How warm it must feel, the light of a soft woman.

All I hear is the thump of the drummer man -
drummer who drummed my child fevers,
drummed the fear into me like nails.

Tonight I admire the vodka's elecricity;
sense each inch of home blindfold -
trail in the death hours of night the prints
of my fingerends slowly
along the wall's fences and hillocks,
over the pyramid switch:
breathless, twist a wrist and open

to the smell of your warmth,
sizzling fresh as a farmhouse breakfast:
I nuzzle beside you, dive into dreams
where the drummer is silenced by your sighs:
where, crowned by suns, we bask
in our wild and tended garden,
scatter light like seeds.

Ted Hughes Meets The Dalai Lama

after Hughes' "Famous Poet"

Look at the old boy: even my
Barbed clauses struggle to
Harpoon just what it is that
They call god.   Those swollen jowels,
   Receding shaven hair,

And the smile of a
Gardener - a propagator, perhaps,
Of obscurer plants amongst the botanists at
Kew: he seems a deer stunned by headlights,
   But I cannot be sure.

I look to the eyes
For the laser drill: but no.   Only
The smile of an Eskimo returning
With the seal.   He bows to me
   Like a fishing rod to the sea.

Is it the studied humility of a man
Ripped from birth into duties for swarms
Of parasitic wasps as they suck out
His light from the inside?
   Or is he just not very clever?

In fact - I hesitate
To tell it straight in this strange,
Glaring light - he is not just monk and
King but maybe almost this:
   Once, the Holy men

By windbells in the altitudes
Bowed before him in their robes,
Anointed him with a child's sacred love
And stomaching the snow at his
   Tiny feet, they prayed.

As a boy it seems
He learned to sow his light and praise:
He cannot hate and has forgotten how to
Curse the selfish or the bayonet:
   Just look! Everyone seems to love him,

Loves him so
As some gentle god who can bless
The darkest of hearts with gifts of light.
I can feel my fame and my iron trail
   Incinerating in the bliss of his love.

Lakeside Inn

Thank God for water, and for the birds that swim upon it.
Among deep concrete corridors, this is a a rare haven.
A fallen leaf scratches across the abrasions of a slab:
something has broken in two.

The sun struggles to warm me,
though magnifies with ease the internet intricacy
of a lacewing: millions of years of daddy long legs
limb by limb by limb, torn.

And the worlds come tumbling down: the biblical colours
fallen into a minestrone of blood, brick and black.

I breathe in stabs, breathe out the pain of others
who have seen the light of friends go out;
where smiles were I see the blood of gums,
the splintered fangs of the wounded.

The mallard's dark jade is iridescent -
its rituals seem ceaseless, its paddlings praise:
I am here to do the same - why else but a quest to see,
to be more giving of this sparse joy?

But what of you; can you limp across such twisting worlds?
If we listen to the mallard, the sorrow cannot crush us.

The lake ripples flame.

You'd call this a diamond day: there should be
the chuckling of love and the blaze of together.

The lake is my breathing:
my breathing is this lake.

This is the first of many sorrows.
This is the first, and this is the last.

There is no fiercer battle -
the sorrow and the fire -

no fiercer battle.

Eden

It is yours, if you want it.

I am already enough,
  And always have been.
I am with you
  Though I may be far from you.
I give you everything
  And insist on nothing.

It is yours, if you want it.

There is so much to become -
  Windows to open,
  Mountains to move,
  Storms to still
  And seeds to sow.

You may understand everything
  When you are ready.

Would you put fire in the hand
  Of a newborn child?

Who would spend his life
  Teaching elephants to fly?

As everything moves,
  So you will move.

My gift is everywhere,
  Not so hidden.

My gift is here -
  You.
    This breath.

      These ears.

It is yours, if you want it.

III Horse Whispering
   In The Military Industrial Complex

God is subtle, but not malicious
EINSTEIN

A man's life of any worth
is a continual allegory
KEATS

Vote

War is a war of what you would die for: love evolving, nature overcoming nature. But we are the prey of desire of the day, the keep-you-angry newspapers; imprisoned in a skull, fearful of all fundamentalists, foreigners, next door neighbours. We live to complain in late night emails or on tiny soapboxes in the comfort of our own virtual home, voting once every five years for this lie or that deception.

Vote with the rhythm of your time and the healing in your hands. Vote with nothing but the truth, the language of autumn leaves, the storm before the calm. Leave blank the reverence for the journalist, celebrity, the gadget, television. And why fill in the box beside *origin*? Simply fill the air with the curved resonance of tabla and dulcimer, kalimba, ney and mandolin; the understanding after a triangle is struck....

Put all your thinking to one side for the child whose eyes are talking in questions, but whose mouth is a fishing boat stranded in mud, waiting for the tide of your patient listening. The war is a war of what you would die for.

Vote with your fingers, your burning mind. Wrap yourself in semtex, in electrical wire, fuses and detonators; wrap yourself in the high explosives of Love: then with a great prayer, blow yourself up and everything with you. Blow up the hoarding and the legalese, the greed and the clinging, the shut-out clauses and the gossip, the too far-gone-to-cares and I-can't-do-thats, the love of only the likeminded and the remote control. See the smithereens of what we all thought so important. And as the air slowly clears, a breeze like wisdom finds new space to breathe, to breathe of the suicide of love, to breathe and walk like more-than-men past our broken nature into the radiant human nature that will outshine everything you've ever feared.

Vote for something bigger than fear and words and knowing. Vote for questions in your answers. Vote for something more subtle than voting. Say yes to listening to the music of your neighbour: how many languages can you laugh in? How many languages can you die in? Say yes to living - and dying - for Love.

Raven

Raven listens to the dead leaves sing;
frost is dripping from his wing.

Still as stone in storm's wild eye
raven hears the thaw's dark cry.

Black and starless, raven and me -
puzzled by song, not yet free.

Mourning the frost, its perfect white:
falling from whiteness, falling from light.

Perhaps, like me, the raven grieves
to hear the thaw fall on the leaves.

Black and starless, raven and me -
puzzled by song, not yet free.

The Rock-Me Timing Bang

Acoustic tuning-seers, here's the rock-me timing bang!
It's like erogenous cinematics, or intravenous slang -
It's a slam in the roll and the scream in the fall
Or the telescopic purity of a starlit crystal ball

That reads the ley-lines through the on-lines
Where the rhythm seeks sublime...
Or sees the white cliffs shatter in the clatter
Of a time whose chime isn't chaste, which flatters

The cut-and-paste method; where-the-predator-is-chased
Method; "his tale is a waste" method; til the facile are faced
By the green cries of felicity and the gold tribes of the free
Just as the sun wakes, singing *wedlock isn't padlock, so be*

Glad of motherbabe and the soul says Yes, the whole will bless
W for Word, so you'll not fall down the professor-hole, the cold chess
Of the mind's endgame: you're here to find the way through,
The flipside breakthrough of me and you (the original version)

Before the subversion of flow. the go. stopped. by inhibitors.
Pharmaceutical do-not-enter-the-centres, the velociraptors
Of your holy soulstrings, as the men who think they own love
Don rubber gloves for the inner inspection. Yes, introspection doves

Will section you, and sever the connection between me and you
Who are one body, but defeatable in parts: their mind is a ruse
For vivisection, so stay alive! walk out of the cage, feel the light -
Rage of the sage say the slang of the timing bang's not over quite

Yet, because the epigram of hexagrams is what I am
And twenty grams of who I am will say to all the radio hams
Don't split it up or the heart will jamjamjamjamjamjam jam

And go! with the fireflow of go river flow-river go
River flow and melt the/melt the/ glacial snow, so
Your truth and your truth and your truth will know...

Becoming
For Victor

The best way is simplicity.
Move yourself out of the way,
And the word floods the ditty.

Let God choose the channels.
The middle's defined by the edges
So climb out, put up the solar panels

And hook up to real sky TV.
It's simple, but not easy, the way:
Becoming what your heart sees.

Neuromemo

Lonely. Skin. Dust.
Light. Lips. YES!
No, must be careful.
One old whisper on the network tube
these days and you're downstream.

I know. I know I'll have to sink this
but how slippery the old therapies feel
sliding over rapids, over the obscene megaliths
of the data genome.

I wish. Yes, I wish they hadn't rained
on all the old windows: what a view
of blossom bees from the french doors
and the labyrinths of lichen cities!

These wires must look like bindweed in the laser light.
I remember. I remember the pearled webs weaving,
weaving their wonder in the infinite inside.

Infinity, finity... this darkness is finity all right.
I hope I've lit up a few of the old frequencies.
Perhaps this phosphorescence will
brand itself onto a rare breeze, find other worlds
like our dreams were, paths on the inside
where the light is still connected,
where they're still hopeful for the hidden brain,
still inspired about the marvels of the double helix.
Who am I now? I'm black as an eyesocket
nailed into their dark dream.

I wish. I wish I could remember anger, or the bump
of my Adam's apple trembling on the stage.
There's no gold in this silence
and they drown all the people dreams.
Who was it who cried to dream again?

I used to sing what I mean
Think think think think NO

YES, I remember -
I remember being woken once...
there was an audience

Dragon Song

Pinocchio has a nose
But I've an honest tail:
With every breath of truth
I grow an extra scale.

People call me reptile
When they see my glistening scales,
But then I breathe from my heart;
It never, ever fails.

A blowtorch of flame
Comes flooding from my lips:
But then everyone starts to think
Of caves and chains and whips.

St.George! St.George, you coward!
You told the world a lie.
You forgot to tell the English
That I can never die.

So what, I loved a virgin -
But she loved me -
She loved my cave of secrets
And the underground sea.

St.George, St.George we begged you
To come into the cave -
We would have shown you all the secrets
And the power that you crave.

But you sharpened up your lance
And you drove it through my heart;
You thought it was all over,
But that was just the start

Because I met her on the firebridge
So radiant and so wise -
You couldn't make her happy,
So you cut her down to size -

But can you see her dancing now
From your ordered fields below?
She's the brightest in the East
With her songs like falling snow.

Through the dark I follow her,
I am her blazing tail.
I follow her silent music
On the very highest scale -

And if you listen in the night
In your deepest, darkest hour
You'll hear her whispers ringing
In the old belltower

And then you'll hear her in the street
And you'll hear her in the trees
And you'll hear her in the tug of sails
On high English seas

And you'll hear her in a friend
And you'll hear her in my cry -
St.George, I have to tell you
That your dragon cannot die.

I am the wings inside you
I'm the tongue within the fire
And the thermals of my breath
Will always take you higher

Because, with her, I blaze the firebridge
To the source of everything -
I am the firebridge in your heart.
I'm the song that you will sing.

God Explains The Poet's Task

When your cells become suns,
Burn the mind of the waiting world.

When your shoulders redden
And become wings you will be
The dragon, though the fire is mine.

Cities will run from you, but the land will thank you.
Love will always admire you, but the ashen
Will try to bury you with their envy.

Listen at the heart of the sun
To the beat of your own nature.

Turn the wires of man into veins of fire -
Transmission is the way, a burning
Passed from one heart to another.

Listen to me always:
I am the heart of the fire.
Everything is changed through me.

No heart or mind can be itself
Unless it moves through me.

I ask only that you accept my gifts
And dazzle the proud, cell by cell;
Turn them to suns to shine beside me.

Follow this path and you will be me.
Another language awaits you then,
Which you may, for now, call light:

But it is more, even as the hymn
Is more than the hiss, or the poem
More than the crumbling glacier.

The Awakening Of The Tribe

In the dark and beery silence, something tribal.
I could sense it in their bellies, something tribal.
I knew what they had come for -
I saw the iron bar -
I smelt the life unspoken, something tribal.

My sister sat so silent, but she smelt it.
The roots - rooted tugging - we all felt it.
They had touched her, they had soiled her
And by God these evil worms
Would feel pain - the pain inside - as they had dealt it.

So simply my father said
The adult words "Now go to bed".
So many times he'd walked blindfold past it -
Past the cropped heads, the slurred threats,
Just for us.   But this was different.
Only the old ways would do now.

Thirty male bellies full of stout.
One little sister full of pain.
Eight cropped heads laughing loud.
Only the old ways would do now.

A gathering of purpose, something tribal.
The iron bar of vengeance, something tribal.
My father simply knew, knew exactly what to do:
The old, old justice, something tribal.

There are orders, there are rules, something tribal.
There are lovers, there are fools, something tribal.
And in folding back the years I see folding back my fears
Thirty stout-breathed vigilantes, marching tribal.

There are limits, there are bonds:
Iron bars, not magic wands -
And my father put things straight,
Something tribal.

I never even ask how they set about the task,
How they beat the rod of justice on that night.
But I know that when they set upon the table in the night
That iron bar in light
That it was bent -
That the old ways had put my sister right.

And God forbid I ever lose the old ways of truth
Drumming like iron bars onto damned flesh;
Neither lose my strong and silent brothers
Coming together in a great gathering -
The gathering of justice, truly tribal.

The Divided City

As long as anyone can remember
The city has been divided.

On the Western side the lanes and laws are straight;
Windows and roofs wear their geometry sharp.
Men and women walk at pace in uniforms
Past miming traders selling clockwork toys.
In the stillness of their eyes, no stars shine.

On the Eastern side the roofs are curved
And all the windows open; the dirt
Falls haphazardly on sleeping dogs
As the shoeless children chase a wheel:
The old man stares, as if hypnotised.

The two sides rarely speak
Unless young lovers cross the unseen line
As every year they seem to do,
And the fathers raise their voices
And their fists as mothers weep:
The priests proclaim and condemn
And recall the first spilling of blood.

The feuding has dug so deep
The only barrier anyone can see
Is the invisible one between them.
Meanwhile the real city wall
Seems always to have been there,
And for all the talk of history
Few can remember who built it.
Fewer still know of the old city gate
Or that those who enter can never be the same.

Overgrown and forgotten in no-man's land,
Only the lovers dare to seek it out,
Magnetised by the tug of their dreams -
On the starless night of no return
The lovers follow their heartbeat to the gate
And ghost through, past the perfumed weeds
And the dust of year-old nests
As lizards rattle through the fallen leaves.

A sudden gust removes the veil of sky
And stars pour blessings down;
The slow meeting of young lips
Is the lighting of a new path
For lovers of all ages -
And what an awakening there would be
In the city tonight if the sleepers saw
The feuds of the past and the dreams to come
Dissolve as one in the Eden of a kiss.

Ding Dong Dung

The universe is speaking
In the human tongue
As the scarab beetle
Rolls its dung

The webs of stars
And rocks in springs
Are where
Imagination sings

And soon the song
Is felt by Light
As galaxies tickle
The cheek of night

Back and forth
The music goes
The strings vibrate
The power flows

And so the scarab beetle
Rolls its dung
And the universe speaks
In the human tongue

Antennae

Twitching for morsels of prophecy,
Feeling for water like a diviner with his rod,
Listening in to the tune of things to come:

Poets are the antennae of evolution....
Eve-olution? Didn't *Adam* have a say?

Yes, *he* nicked the apple and blamed it all on her!

OK, evolution with a little RRRRR -
A kind of motorbike tiger high rev thing:

Give evolution an R.....   aaaaaaah!
The Sabre-toothed Bambi paradox...
There is mercy in the nature of man.

Yes, give evolution an R and you spell Revolution -
So...revolution's just evolution speeded up a bit,
Evolution with more revs -

It's a sink-or-swim-no-time-to-lose-to-save-civilisation situation!

Reinsert the feathers of mercy in your shoulderblades
Or every tower's going nine eleven -
No more seventh heaven masculine/feminine tightrope walk
Lighting up the backbone of the acoustic temple body -

Just the million-bucks-a-throw Cruise missiles screaming
My God kills quicker than yours

...Don't remember the commandment
About stripping off your brother's skin
And hanging him up at the butcher's
With a metal hook the shape of an S through his mouth -

Ssssss...   Behind you!   The bad guy's behind you
Like a shadow: they do a good job with fear,
It's their expertise - teasing the love out of you
Like a silver hook flashing in the sun
That just ripped you out of the water -

They'll let you slap around on the wet deck,
Insane for breath under a laughing sun

Before they tear your innards out
And bury you in ice!

But the book knows; the look knows,
The rook in the rookery nook knows,
The nose knows, the rose knows,
The toes in the blowing sand know

That breath is our signature spiralling
Through the revolution of a moment
Where we exchange lightning like kisses

Just as the night antennae
Of the stars stretch out
Vibrating through spacetime
Like music.

News

The news is always arriving out of silence RILKE

Passion is the new cool
A hunch is the new rule
Listening is the new speed
Breath is the new seed

Love is the new rage
Music's the new word
Live is the new page
Truth is the new sword

Repetition's the new freeform
The edge is the new norm
Idea is the new thing
Release is the new cling

Vibe is the new heart to heart
Arise is the new fall
The whole is the new part
Singularity the new all

Fingers are the new wings
Grace is the new advertising
A gift is the new thief
Faith is the new belief

Touch is the new Zen
Soul is the new science
Now is the new then
Poetry is the new silence

Page & Stage

How do you scan your fingers?
And what do you mean by those eyes?
I missed the bit you said just now.
I detest this constant surprise!

Please write it down on some paper
Then type it up nice and neat
Then send it off to be published
And *then* I can hear the beat

and the breath and the death of the wings by the nail that sings like a jackboot:
Judas, you thought you'd sort it with your dosh and pulling strings, playing it rough
but we are such stuff as schemes like yours fade upon like butter in the wok;
Dr Spock would've been proud of you, but the spirit growled at you,
and you strung yourself up for the barking in your head: there's no larking
with the dead, but if Judas sang on the melody of the resurrection boomerang,
you'd hear behind the hellfear the heaven-clear *if only: if only I had heard then
the breath of a monarch's wing, the sing my studies never heard, the world
of the pearl thing* welcome to the lightning of fire and ice, splicing beatitude into
the attitude of the platitude, the blessing before the bang, stressing not where
the egomoney's taken us, but the might of who we might be if your heart has not
forsaken us; and are we so mistaken, we who love with our fingers and love with
our eyes, who prize the surprise of the breath and the power greater than death
that cannot be nailed down?

The Painter's Odyssey

For Hugo & Sophie Grenville

His eloquent pictures of silent dreams
Invite us to a revelation - clouds
Part in our eyes; in Straits of sun, sea-streams
Flow to the whip of a whirl where crowds
Of sailors drown in roaring foam with cries
Of hell and home. To avoid this killer
Water, our captain seeks the other side,
Bravely to face the six-headed Scylla,
Whose butcher teeth mince bones to mash. Narrow
Is the path between - and no sooner past,
Than Siren-spells calling him like a rose.
But he already knew - tied tight to the mast,
Deaf to their song, his eyes blaze back the sky:
Its colours reveal all that light must say.

Horse Whispering in the MIC

We got divorced from the horse, so now we're the cart leading - everything's fine
Doctor, apart from this strange wooden feeling - Did I ever suggest that the best
method's breathing? But we're underwater with the sharks, gobbling blood in the
harbour dark and with all these bitemarks in the wood, we could be sinking the
ark! Try thinking pink like a flamingo, you won't sink when you let your wings go
and you won't wink as you whisper all you know; because everything flows. So
wonder and wander as you would in the weird wild wood where the owl's howling
like a wolf and there's a cleft in your hoof and Peter Pan is breathing fire like the
dragon of truth; but if they can't stop the flames, they'll slice his head off as proof!
They bring out the least in us to bring out the beast in us
They use their minds on us to blind us to the heart of us

Everyone got splashed by the Big Brother pool - soon they'll be saying
snuff movies aren't cruel - all empires are fuelled by divide and rule. Hide
your big side or they'll find it and use it against you: they enter placentas to
feed all the children an excessive percentage of longing and hatred! But
when you play trains in the attic the big sky is static, and Daddy's less
manic, remembering his childhood and the fur in his hood: the kingdom
never leaves you, it's easier to be true: look, it just flew in pixel by pixel,
this fine flaming phoenix should easily fix this; but they say that landing
is tricky because there's no aerodrome: the meaning gets mixed up
on military phones
They bring out the least in us to bring out the beast in us
They use their minds on us to blind us to the heart of us

Now the winged horse is landing, standing on our screen: why the military parade
then, and the loaded magazines? The big idea has always been fear; pedal that and
we'll get you all the gear: we'll get you the polar bear coats and some coke in your
goatee for some suicide boats and the votes of the bloated; because they'll make
you *long* for a piece of it - they'll start a little war, sell more arms, offer you the
golden fleece for it: the more we buy for buying's sake the harder we squeeze the
trigger of our piece for it: the barrel of the gun rests on the temple of love for it -
take off your glove, you're not an assassin! When they're asking you why, will you
say it was the gun that squeezed you? While the sun is still free, take a ride on
the wild horse in you
Then you'll harvest the feast in us and the rising like yeast in us
As we're turning the mind of us to ride back to the heart of us

Fourteen Week Scan

Wake up! Wake up!
The ultrasound is calling.

From your dark sea cell
You sing back all the details
Of your seethrough inner life -

The discs of your spine
Like an open zip -
Candlestick fingers -
The hemispheres of your brain
Perfectly bisected by a tightrope;
That narrow path you'll balance on,
Clinging to our fingers.

Your beating heart, a dancer.
Your tiny stomach, militant in the making.
Your mother smiling, her cheeks on fire,
Imagining the first page of your album.

And with the whispered words
"The three of us" we walk out
Into the trinity of a November sun
Dancing in the silence, hand in hand,
Dreaming of the light on your fingers.

The Weavers

Love needs lovers -
There are no horrors there.

There are many rooms:
Do not clear out the spiders
Who have dreamed you.

You are caught in a web
Called the real: love is hungry -
She needs lovers to weave
Her wonders in the wild places.

The horror
Is watching from the outside:
The weaving
Comes from within.

The silk is strong as love -
It unfurls, spinning out
From a dark knot into the light,
Flinging itself fearless between stars,
Healing the old rip in the fabric
That is you, dizzy in the spinning.

Spinning should be slow -
A hurricane needs an eye -
A howling music in the silence
Between this and that silence,
This and that weaving

The web of a new believing
Conceiving the new weavers,
The believers of song,
The longing a reaching, breaching
The old: opening the untold,
Listening to the quiver of the web
Ringing with the struggle of this time

As together we dream and build
And never cease the song of love
To inspire the peace.

St.George's Day

I'm proud to admit - gosh - aren't you proud to be Bobby Charlton
Mini Cooper Monty Python? To be alive in this green and pleasant
mad mix of Murray Walker Lenny Henry Robin Hood
Leaves On The Line Stonehenge E-Type Jaguars Marmite The Clash?!
This Michael (or Wilfred) Owen Johnny Rotten Camilla Charlie
Paul McCartney Barmy Army Ode To A Nightingale -
Vindaloo. Ecowarriors. Sol Campbell. Vivienne Westwood.
Darwin Shelley Newton Wembley creative and financial
Bobby Moore of The Globe?

Oh the real ale Frank BrunoWimbledon queues Ted Hughes
The Great Bard's Well 'ard Vinny Jones The Rolling Stones
Avebury Middle Order Batting Collapse Bohemian Rhapsody Chaps!
Page 3 Rolling Hills Satanic Mills Last Of The Summer Wine I May Be Gone
Some Time Poor Old Toad Wrong Kind Of Snow Quiet Desperation....Help
me Out O Corporation... 7.13 to Waterloo Station of it all....

This realm of Cod n' Chips Mr.Bean Johnathon Woss
Wall's Ice Cream Marquee Weddings. The Beano!
Bluebells Churchbells 180! Swing Low Sweet Chariots Of Fire.
It's The Taking Part - It's The Taking Apart!
Goodness Gracious Me BBC OBE I'm free! Three Lions On A Shirt
Strawberry Fields Forever TransientTranceRaveTechnoTrainspotting
Welcome To The House Of Fun And The Drugs Don't Work
Tallyho Dallaglio! But the Wonderful Thing About Tiggers is
Magic Roundabout Hedgerows and Chainsaws Brixton Riots
Tellytubbies The JamTheJam Ordering Organic Cucumbers
On the Internet Camelot's a Lottery and the winner is...
Stephen Lawrence's Mum and Dad's Army The Dark Side
Of The Mooning Out Of Cars Gary Numan - The Numinous!

Imagine All The People - Living Life - Beyond National Identity!
The You & Me Connected Beyond National Identity (Everybody
Needs A Bosom For A Pillow) - the All Admitted No Exclusions
Of You & Me watching those Feet in Ancient Times Walk upon
England's mountains green or, Silver in the Lake, Excalibur!
And Arthur whose Hand takes the Sword like a Thorn
From your Heart Round Table Fresh Start - To Be Or
Not To Be The Example Of Nations? Defenders Of Faith
Always Look On The Bright Side Of
Chaos /Order /Chaos /Order /Duality /Unity /Order
Butterfly Wingbeat Of The Individual Gesture...
Why Leave That Candle Unlit?

Left Right Middle Path!
Sprinting Along The Fence To The Golden City.
Egg Sperm
Miracle Of Life!

You May Say I'm A Dreamer -
Milton Blake Jonny Wilkinson -
but I'm not the only one -
And aren't you proud to be -
the Power of You & Me!
nor shall our swords sleep in our hands -

Alive in the Living Word of the Here & Now,
The Beat of the Burning Heart
Blazing Once More In the Deep
As The Lightning Seeds Burst
And Scatter a Bright New Hope
In this Happy Mixed Breed of Emerging Gods
Awaking new-inspired at last
Upon this Precious Earth,
This Blossoming Realm,
This Wild & Holy Rose Garden Of An Island...
This *England!*

By Chance

The honoured calculations of Genesis
have come my way, quite by chance.
I have gambled in the crystals
of another language, and found it:
the broken tablet makes sense
like dreams do, if you let them.

Angels do not jeer at the mystery
of our ignorance. They envy us.
We have the freedom to dive
through the esoteric sublime roots
they are forced to cling to.

So do not jeer at ignorance.
Like chance, it sings to the unknown.

And the honoured calculations of Genesis
assure me I can only begin
once I know nothing.

Apparently we all have it,
as we all know how to smile.

Please honour this simple calculation.
Make space in your own myth.
For in the spring of chance
I found this, freshly scrolled.

Virtual Games

You must watch the killer whales snaking
across the dunes: records may well be broken.
There should be some close fights this year:
the komodo dragons have started breathing
mustard gas - and the hammerheads
have a new chainsaw attachment.

The praying mantis are big enough for the buffalo now
and there's good odds on a decapitation in one.
I think I'll avoid the mangling this year; the liquidiser pit
is messy at best, and the blood paintings too vivid for comfort.
Just reminds me of the first games: it was the last bell;
they hooked out one of the old-style humans from the pit.

He didn't thank us though, just started chanting
some drummer mumbo-jumbo, holding up
his fingers as if they were the ten wonders of the world.
How we laughed as he was lowered into the fire.
But my blood went slow because I saw something...
something inside and outside, clear as a dream -

As if the man was burning through my visor
and my eyes were fire for an instant and I saw
oceans of whales and trees with leaves and I was the man
and the man was a tree growing towards the sun
and everything was laid out before me
in this beautiful golden web -

But I'm sure the games will charge us up again.
And the reality is sure to be entertaining.
Forget the burning man. Delete him!
One little tap of a key and he'd be gone.
But I can't bring myself to do it.
I just can't.

Nature Poem

If I was writing this Nature's way
It would have to be grand and cryptic:
I'd cut root and mammal shapes into these pages
And furl them up, crumpled as mountains.
Then from the origami range
I'd pattern letters so vast
You could read the clues from Mars.

The pattern would take lifetimes
To shape, journeys through the secret land
Of dreams and the libraries of Man -
Yet even if I saw through a thousand eyes,
Past vales of death and judgment fields,
Through prophets' minds, and angels' too -
What words can say why Nature moves,
Why cells begin and planets die?

And even if revelation spoke in flame
From the sanctum in the far deep,
It wouldn't use our human tongue
But would hold up our hearts like a mirror to the sun -
And we would shine in the language of shining.

Something is stirring, outside speech.
I hear an orchestra rattle like tinnitus -
A sudden sun blasts me with silence -
And I know that shining is a language,
Shining is Nature's most sacred song.

The Journey of the Law

*The way of poetry extends unaltered
to the final age*   Saigyo

You have lain down
In a cold silent crypt
And walked for days
Among dragonflies.

You have followed
The silent beat
Of the golden deep
In your innocence.

You have listened
To the birdsong pollen
Gasping through the leaves
Of clenched trees.

You have fallen
And have asked for help
From the subtle light
Of the morning star

128

And now you know
You must learn a new law
In the cooling rings
Of the living flame

And you can hear
The chanting tide
Between the sounds
As the love crashes in

And from the secret circles
Of the central fire
You send back word,
Your long fingers of light

Clasping the palms of the dark
Pulling it up to the fire
To resume its living purpose
In the holy choir of stars.

Harvest

Under the tinroof sweat of summer
Straw rained in the dark stack
As the red tractor rattled in once more
With sixty-four bales in its teeth.
And back for more, and more,
The tractor's roar strident, then dying
To the coiled hiss of the straw
As dust bit into burned skin.
In pauses of drying sweat
The silence spat venom in my eyes.

But the last day was different.
Six harvest men on a trailer
Hurling bales eight high,
Dreaming of the first ale of evening;
Jack's toothless whistle and the Cortina he rebuilt
Every year, failing to haul a caravan to Cornwall;
Chris with his unstringed bale of hair,
His guitar cottage on the dark side of the moon;
The boss, Hammer Sarge, so abrupt and kind,
And his redhead son, at first afraid to laugh;
And Archie, the Yorkshire barrel of beer,
A joyride of quips and tales and hidden pain.

And each bale we heaved we praised
In the first pints of earth and gold
That harvest evening. Each pain we sank,
Each smile we soaked as drips cooled exhausted lips,
Sang in our throats as the tales grew tall.

And yet it's the red teeth of the tractor
That haunt me, and the lonely sting
Of the dark heat away from the singing sun;
And I think of a working man
And his dream for his child
Who he prays will never be a slave
To the piston and the lathe;
Who will know the brave stories of ale,
And the golden straw flying through laughter
At the harvest's end.

Home Truths

The twilight is nothing
if it cannot teach us;
the far truths must find
their way into our little gestures;

the squeeze of a hand,
you smiling by the windswept river.

The stars are no brighter
than neon if they cannot tell us
their tales of light and dust,
or confess their candle-like fragility.

Even the rose is incidental red,
some empty stain

unless as gift or memory of love
we hold it taut-stalked between the thorns,
the folds of perfumed red
a spiralling perfection
of parallel and perfect worlds

where our love
and these stars
on still nights like this

rush me to the heart of bliss
in the warmth of your fragile palm.

Awake

I am standing in the lucid dream
Of your life. To wake up
In the middle of your dream,
Speak now: say I AM AWAKE.

Those who wake are the seeds
Of the storm of the time to come.

You are the carpenters of the ark,
Those who know the things of true value
And what must be saved.

I am the voice of the lucid dream
Of your life. If you need to know
The path, listen truly in the deep.

Listening is a matter of life and death:
What you do here matters.

Why curse the darkness when history has left
A box of matches in your pocket?

There is meaning in your pain.
You are studying the wrong side
Of the tapestry. You curse needle
And scissors, deny the pattern.

Wake up and walk round
To view the full picture
Of the tapestry of your life.

Who's that bright figure in the corner,
Kneeling by the river?

The mind asks questions
Only the heart can answer.

Wisdom says
There is only one tapestry
Though it has two sides.

Wisdom says
There is one truth
Though there are many dimensions
Of waking and sleeping.

Wisdom says
Move forward, leave
Your shadow behind you.

Wisdom says
Walk back to the sun
And all will be well.

Everybody Wants To Be

Everybody wants it all: name in lights, cracking the highs and avoiding the fights;
but we're bang in the bad man's sights - we're his fly-by-wire for his 9-11 nights:
it's all take, Mr.Flake, and our makeover outside is his takeover inside - he lies
about *everything* and now we're hiding it - it's all sliding in, so wake up! You called?
… He stalled. Let's just call this gliding - mine's a Stella - I like your
timing - now where's that starman fella hiding?

It won't be long now, feel the spirit in this song now, it's time for The Holy Land to
flow and get along now: the prophets have gone quiet (should be starting a riot): see
the haloes, they fly out like Frisbees at Christmas, this isn't their business, so whose
rhythm is this? Beyond all their schisms, their ists and their isms, we're standing
like prisms, so one light becomes…many colours! You Hindu purple, me Buddha
brown; you Jewish country, me Muslim town; you Christian serious, me Dervish
clown - it's time to get down, attach paradise feathers in the wildest of weathers,
the spirit's not tethered, they'll never forget us!

Everybody wants to be like Jesus, so please us, unfreeze us, we're orange, so
squeeze us; she's love, she won't tease us - show her wings, she'll release us!

The Old Testament's yesterday, the tests are meant for today where we pray for
the Father but which would he rather? Walk out of the old talk and sing like Bjork!
We're chalk dust? You cannot be serious! Judas thought that way and hung   133
himself, delirious: the playground bully makes us shiver; the sea does not flow into
the river: God did not invent seeds so he could make us fat off his creed! So let love
off her leash, hear the shells on the beach, the river can teach us so I'm watching the
river, I'm watching the river, I'm watching the river flow into the sea….

He wasn't a gangster, he's a trickster, a prankster, a light we all link to, he's every
way through, because that's what the love wants the lovers to do! She loves all the
losers, the boozers and schmoozers, the outsiders, the providers, the big Harley
riders, the hide-from-yourselfers, the stuck-on-the-shelfers, the poor, the sore, the
old lady next door, the rich man who knows what his money is for, the fun man who
can't find his fun anymore, and you - is that the worst you can do? She surely
loves you - your head's a volcano, you'll cook such a brew when you try something
new, so throw out the ash, look around at this glue - stick to the Love and the Love
sticks to you.

Everybody wants to be like Jesus, so please us, unfreeze us, we're orange, so
squeeze us: she's love, she won't tease us - show her wings, she'll release us!

Sorceress

"I am a spring," she says.
"I am the source."

Come down then, down to my river -
flow through me,
trickle through the startled light
of my meadows -
these petals so curved, the pollen so moist.

This sorceress, she moves me.

Slowly she sighs an ember breath.
Fingers curve their grace on flesh
and my smile is sabre tooth
and the beast bends in the deep cavern -

frenzy of fire on flint-cut walls
and my hide is in hackles -
bristle of nerve and sinew
roar of muscle and pulse
then crush of a whisper

and agony -

the dawn sigh.

This sorceress, she moves me.

In the gasp of cooling dew
she turns
and we settle
like hands in prayer
into us.

Hallowed Ground

Can truth, like jewels, be suddenly found?
In a dream the words lit up my mind:
To ignite the fellowship of hallowed ground.

What does it mean, this eerie sound?
Is it Time itself I hear unwind?
Can truth, like jewels, be suddenly found?

Our planet-threads will fray, unwound,
My task, perhaps, to weave and bind,
To ignite the fellowship of hallowed ground:

One day to see the teachers crowned,
The wheelchairs walk, the killers kind:
Can truth, like jewels, be suddenly found?

Our star shines still as we go round
From that vast flame the spark I'll find
To ignite the fellowship of hallowed ground.

In storms of mind we run aground;
To the solar wind still blinkered, blind.
Truth will, like jewels, be suddenly found
To ignite the fellowship of hallowed ground.

The Lodger

I have my very own full-time poet-in-residence.
Wakes me up at all hours singing at the top of his voice
Like he's Maria Callas - or he thinks he's Cecil B de Mille
And there's a full-scale chariot race blasting from ear to ear.

But the silences
Can go on for days and days.
Worries me to death.
Is he dead?

Then wham! he goes all pentecostal
Or hurricane on me at 3am
And the stink of singeing sheets
And ash for a pillow in the morning....

He never knocks - says please -
Or brings a present.
He thinks he's present enough.

Tells me secrets though -
But get the wrong end of the stick
Or stick your oar in before time
And the headaches go on for hours.

Strange business, being a landlord -
Hardly feels like it's my house anymore.
It's not as if he pays me a penny.

Just whispers to follow the poems
Like stepping stones to the other side
And says that should be enough.

I'm not sure I could throw him out.
You never know -
He might be on to something.

There Will Be Poets

a version of Rilke's First Sonnet to Orpheus

A tree is rising, there - it's a miracle!
God sings a tall tree in your ear
And all is still.   In this lyric, all
Begins *now*; all is changing *here* -

Animals from the silence come into the clear
From dens and nests, into the open wood.
It wasn't *guile* that brought them here,
Or let them breathe so softly: they could

Only come to *listen*.   Howls and roars they found
Too limited for their hearts.   And though, before this,
The tiniest hut had held what was heard here -
An airless place of longing and fear
With a rickety old door for an entrance -

Now you build them cathedrals in their sense of sound.

Aragorn's Song For Arwen

I am naked in a warm rain -
You drink me from the spring of my body.

My lips are still for a great movement....

Listen to the love my body whispers -

I am lost in the night of you;
The stars make impossible promises in your eyes -

I am a tear dripping into a well,
Singing of the far rivers and the ways through oceans.

You flow through
My every breath.

Sometimes you're a sudden wind gathering leaves
And the branches inside me are drumming   -

I go to war for you...

Or I step into a stillness
Of a full moon above a mountain lake -

I cry your name above the forests!

I will not let the sky forget you -
Not the North Star - nor the crystal streams -

My heart is a rememberer

And you have always been
The pulse in my midnight fingers

Cove

Moments before it enters the sea,
The stream is excited -

The afternoon fire in the sky
Makes the streamwater wild with light

Like a huge crowd
Manically waving torches

Or the cities of the world
Turning their lights on and off

Incredibly fast - celebrating a victory
Perhaps, or even a miracle.

The stream is excited
Moments before it enters the sea.

Logos

Logo's a nogo that throws the flow and blows the globe so dough's a dodo so-and-so
disease; please squeeze the trees of all their sap, suck out the fish, hear the food
chain snap, freeze all the love, put desire on tap, keep the good people down in the
poverty trap; I say old chap, do you write to *The Times* with a rap? Or the clap in the
storm of alive is a slap in the face, a star falls for the grief of this place, the future's
bright, the future's blue, what else does Love want you to do? You've got
five seconds to go, you're so wasted crew, no wonder it's sinking the think in your
thinking, they're drinking you dry, first class Martini mile high, telling us we can't
fly *anywhere* without them, I wonder why; but the lie isn't over till the big mama
sings from the white cliffs of Dover of the wings we need to be freed from their creed
they're remixing the love life you really need: listen to the reed bending in the wind;
forgive me mother for I've been binned, recycle my soul, let me climb to
be whole, all of the time I've been sold and I thought Red Bull gave me -

save me, for Red Bull is what it is, we are the slaves to all this, glued to the
cavewall of all this, this is your call, all of this, watch us all fall in this bliss,
breathe in the call, believe in the leaving all this, love believes in the listening
bliss; time to rewind them and then to remind them that we are all players and
we'll sing our say as we play in the spray as we surf away on the waves of the
star that burns and burns is burning beyond; we must eyeball all of the pike in
the pond; watch the fern turn, learn about spores and the frond; feel our hearts
and minds burn in the core and beyond; we can soar, take the child out of war
to beyond; better jump off the merrygostore, see beyond -

because the sun's just spun in the nogo of the logo, taking a fireblade to the knot of
the flow crew: dadading-batama-batamaloo! we give back your heart, don't let them
brand it, just stand under yes! you can stand it, stand under and you will understand
it! you just hooked a marlin, don't brand it....; you just hooked a marlin in the sun
of the seventh seal, so reel it in, it's something real on the silver hook, reel it in, it's
something you can feel on the silver hook; reel it in, bring it on board; look it in the
eye, see its spike like a sword; look it in the eye, don't let them brand it: look it in
the eye and you begin to understand it; and so you let it go, splashing back into the
nameless burning water

140

Goddess

She keeps the fire alive and knows no lust.
Dust she has seen, but champions the stranger.

Arrange her slowly and love will show you
True as a child, the placenta of truth:
Truth to nourish the unborn world.

Whirled in the pool of her cupped hands
Lands shine apple-still in a sea of glass.

Ask, and her tasks will be assigned you.
Behind you, death swarms - but before
Imploring, you leap bravely out of water's sleep,

Keeping calm, for her breath is starlight:
Knights in a daze are waking at the fall,
Calling to be burned by the breath of her brand
In the land of the star-tongued messengers.

Lock Me In

Lock me in, I don't mind:
This is no punishment.
Perhaps you love the drama
Of the keys, the measured slams.
For me it is music, a tuning up
For the opera you cannot hear.

I do not fold myself up on my bed
Like a foetus in the dark sea.
I pause and gaze at the window,
Opening like a porthole.

Its opening is my ritual
And climbing out my courage
Til I stand on the roof
As a child of the sky
Where the clouds have no keys
And the invisible stars
Are diamonds hiding in the darkness
Of my little room

And though it is day they sparkle now
And I can see squirrels fly in moonlight
And porpoise surf in the tanker waves
And I can see the storm of my mother's face
Calm to a smile.

Lock me in, I don't mind.
I don't believe you mean me harm.
If you really wanted to punish me
You'd take away the sky.

Walk Out

Walk out of the house of time.
Walk through the paper screen of space.
Behind the party lights of stars
The fire burns without a face.

Though it is far, it is near.
It will melt your iron mind.
Much mightier than you dreamed,
But not impossible to find.

Watch your paper words in fire
How they incinerate to gold:
You are burning all your books
In the tale that can't be told.

Only then will you breathe again
In the music of the fire
And the golden dance will take you up
To the last ecstatic choir

And your wings in bliss will stretch
And the song of songs unfold
A symphony of blossoming
The libretto of the rose

And the cells ignite like stars
And the love like light is spread
Across the lightning circuits
Of the living and the dead

And now the walls have fallen down
And the paper's turned to dust:
The winds are free to take you,
And you must follow. You must.

Rackel & Sangomen
Two Voices From The Inferno

> *The fire that heals*
> *The fire that burns*
> *The world that's still*
> *The world that turns*

flameshrieking blisterburn-infernoburning flameshriekhowl! howlingbrain
tincanbang-tinnitus - fearfear fear i fear voices tintintinbang voices voices
howling cack-cack-cack cacaco-caconoises hackshrieking tinbangtin holocaust
rackrack-blisterscald! flameboil pains ear, painsear, flames that burn! flames
that char charnel-house bone stenchrot-bones! remember vultures bonepick
remember coffin death death-music, music death remember music remember

> The fire that heals -
> Cycles of water, cycles of fire.
> Dragonfly's incandescent bell
> Of river, stream and melody;
> Narwhal's spinning spiral tusk
> Of light and ice and melody.
> I am chained to all life,
> To the beating mind of earth,
> But am a blissful prisoner:
> The songs of trees and mists
> And spider-lines, the music
> Of a gold dune, an oryx
> Sending out the two long shadows
> Of its horns across the jewels of grains,
> The dust our bones become.

remember howl remember banghowl! tortureshriek-spaghettiwire why
machines why wolflasers, mastodon mecanny-canical blinkline-assembly
blink blink doe lightbomb dodo screams like a vixen! razorblade rips
raw-red path across bay-baby's adam's apple - the torture me, the torture
mine! the torture me, the torture mine! remember remembaby blistering
the innocents howl the venom drugged soldiers orders soldiers venom!
electropowermasters, venom! vain vain vein vein-kings, egorambos,
super-robots we decapitated the children we decapitated the children...!

> *The fire that heals*
> *The fire that burns*
> *The world that's still*
> *The world that turns*

You could not hear,
You would not hear.
Now you listen to your pain.
You listen to your pain.
But souls may begin again,
For there is a fire that heals.
If you find the fire inside you
And burn it into swords
You will stand against the torture
As you listen to the children.

but how many years how many how much much inferno-pain and time
time inferno-paintime flametime - the boiling of my ears blisters of my eyes
boiling of my years blisters of my skies scrawling of my lies squealing of the
seers ripping of the flies howling of my fe-

Rackel! Be still.
Be still; be still.
Listen to Sangomen:
In my skies I have
Healing I may breathe.
A chance of reprieve.
Be still. Be still,
Humble and still.

I will muffle all your voices
As you humble, as you still
As you humble, as you still.
In your silent heart be still.

The fire that heals
The fire that burns
The world that's still
The world that turns

Rackel, dear Rackel,
You were still once
In the music of your heart.
Let me remember for you,
Let me remember
How we were still.
In the sky of our minds once
We knew no prisoners,
No prisons and no torture.
We knew only the voices

Of the wise dead,
The truth of innocence,
The candle of a child
Before the painting
Of a whitebeard under the sun.

My tears, dear Rackel,
Carry the lightning of ecstasies -
The bliss-balm of the fire-rose
Blossoming in the blind gardens
Of the inner veils
Of the lovers' red.

Dear Rackel, be still.
Let me pour all over you,
All over your pain,
All the light
Of the cooling sun,
Healing as a glacier wall
Against your blistered lips,
Healing as a glacier wall
Against your blistered lips.

The fire that heals
The fire that turns
The world that's still
The world that burns

Wherever You Are

Carry the cities
and the temples
and the streams
in your breath.

Carry the lovers
and the photons
and the falcons
in your fingers.

Carry the rose
and the secrets
and the suns
in your eyes.

Carry the child
and the chrysalis
and the dance
in your smile.

Carry all these things
and you will be carried.

Fire

The heart is nothing but a sea of fire   RUMI

Hypnosis dances your eyes
back to the beginning.
The fallen oak flares
its last golden message:
There is a love
that burns us into love.

Fire changes everything.
The darkness cowers, breathes
its last ashen breath,
for we can suspend fire
like suns for more lives
than we can think of.

The stars shine into your heart:
they never let you forget
that you burn to be like them.
Though darkness must come again,
when your doubt is deep enough
all the suns will pour back in.

148

Hands will not blister
when they touch you, but long to be
the supernova you have become,
in your eyes, your slow grace:
you walked through hell: all are
aghast at your unburned lips:

the lips of a child that breathed
whatever was, and the world became.
In the swift hands of the wind
or the curled palm of the waves
the world became, and the child in you
stood naked by the shore.

You walked through the deep burning
gardens, singing of the Age Of Fire, listening
to the fire that roars now in your soul.
Everything is there; or here; between the syllables,
beyond the whispers of meaning;
a new love burning in the silence.

Bwindi Impenetrable National Park

Bwindi. Bwindi.
It means "the place of darkness".
An impenetrable forest of night,
The black hole at the core
Of the heart of darkness.
Bwindi. Bwindi.

Sun turns on the white mist
In the forest mountain dawn.
Silent walkers stride purposefully
Along a rare path - path
Of a thousand machetes,
A path with a heart, to the heart -
To the eyes of the silverback
And the simple secret of ourselves.

Moss has settled on the dangling
Parabola of a vine -
Green settles down with green -
The world is a root and a trunk
And we listen to the sap beating
To the rhythm of the morning.

It's a hard climb to the gorillas' nest,
To the thrones of green.
Here the tribe sat last night
In the thundering darkness,
Lashed by the fury of the drops,
Stiller than we can imagine -
As we sat restless and dumb
Fidgeting with knives and forks,
As the gods nailed down
Our corrugated roof
In a frenzy of irritated drums -

And so the silence here
Of empty thrones
Seems still more silent,
Looking down
On the green crown of the valley.
The silverback would have sat here
Above his tribe

On the green throne carved by his weight,
Breathing his kingdom slowly.

Beside him, untouched -
So close to the might of his black palm -
Two butterfly-shaped pink blooms
Loop upwards on their stems
Like shaving mirrors.
Untouched.

Breathless, we follow the fresh path
To the rustlings and the grunts -
We know they are there, we know -
Then a patch of dark - a sudden star -
An eye! - and she is there,
Her baby on her back -
And he is there - a giant skull
And the world's most arrogant eyes
Set deep in his mind -
The philosopher-king is there,
And now he is stripping the bark -
Bending the branches to him,
Bending his kingdom to his lips.

For an hour we thrill to
The Zen mastery of each gesture
The effortless music of farting
The arrogance of innocence:
The baby at play, learning
To bend the branches.

Their ways have made men listen:
They have been granted a kingdom.
In the foothills of these mountains
Enemies who slice machetes
Into the faces of women and children
Agreed on only this:
The mountain gorilla must be saved.

And then we leave them to their peace,
Suddenly aware of the machetes
That carved this path -
The power of a sharpened blade.

But the midday sun has lit up
Another tribe - the butterflies.

They dance around us like our hopes
And settle in clusters to eat,
Sucking the goodness from the stones.

We walk slower now, with still more reverent care
As everywhere the butterflies dance like confetti
Around us, they dance like praise around us.

So this is Bwindi.   This is the place of darkness.
I ask our guide the local name for light.
"Omushana", he says.

Bwindi   Omushana
Bwindi   Omushana

Omushana

Visitor

A poem is a dream of sound and this is my dream:
I dream of a vast sunbird from Andromeda
Gliding to our planet on the secret
Thermal breath of stars.
The sunbird lands on Madagascar
In a frenzied din of hope and fear. From the cave of its ear,
A figure descends, thin and graceful as an impala,
Its cloak of feathers the colours of fire.
The face is almost human, but shines like a wetsuit.
The eyes are stiller and deeper than a whale's.

In the clash of cameras Earth's great leader
Swells with bearded charisma and points to the sky.
His top scientists have lassoed the moon
And are winching it across for an eclipse, so their visitor
May observe the entire planet lit up by day in neon light.
The visitor takes the leader's hand and hushes him
With his sea-dark eyes.   "Please do not," the visitor whispers.
"Please take me to the edge of your sea, to a place
where only the wind and the waves disagree."
A young scientist with nocturnal eyes knows a place.
"By the desert. The Skeleton Coast."

The young man takes them there and under the first stars
The three men sit crosslegged in the sand,
Looking out at the skeletons of battered ships,
Listening to the tale of the wind and the waves.
"In your loud world" the visitor begins, "I must tell you this."
"The knowledge that will save you lives in sound. All the love,
The truth of happiness: all is hidden in natural sound."

Wave after wave falls in the night.

"But what about silence?" the young man asks.

"The greatest secrets of all are hidden
In the ultrasound of silence.
The power that fuels the brightest stars burns there."

"But what must we do?" the leader asks.

"We shall wait patiently for the dawn,
And listen to the songs of the light."

The Great Rift Valley

Vultures stare down on the great valley.
The first pillar of sky fell here,
left its print as long as Africa.

On the plains below zebra kick dust into the shadows
as evening broods, pregnant with rain. Gazelle hairs stiffen
ready for the fall, but a seventh sense alerts the vultures
to a deeper darkening: they steal away in shrieks beyond the clouds

as lightning lurches with bent claws,
sizzling its pain like the death chair: thunder cracks
like test tubes pressed too far: lions convulse,
wild tongues frothing with twisted chemistries:

flung down from darkness vast webs of wires, chains
and cables writhe and clasp the valley edges,
clamping their suckers like tapeworm, heaving the edges in:
in the madness of shadows zebra gnash through their own
hooves, teeth racing like chainsaws: gazelles sprout fangs,
rip apart their young as the valley sides bulldoze closed
in ending's roar like the Red Sea roaring in.

Wires winch to final tightness like vagina lips stitched.

Last little lumps of earth teeter into the slit, nearly silent.
From an edge two dying zebras limp out
like insects from death's demented lips:
into the hell-dark mouth the vultures swoop
feasting in the deep dark on bent meat and baked blood:

soon bloated, lonely in the dark circles of their tribe,
they flap awkwardly between the silent carcases,
remembering wings wide as the world -
the brightness of blood in the sun -
dreaming of what the first pillars held high.

If Everyone Did

Let's have a scrap!   let's do a   *rap*!
          or sscratch the ssilence ....
    a hip   a hip   a hip   a hip hop !

    - but hey now whoa!   I gotta stop -
          cos I'm white -   this ain't right -
        an' I don't say ain't -   it's too   quaint -
I gotta apply   some   fresh paint
    to this great rhythm   poetry
          this great   rhythm   poetry -

  now let's see -   there's you out here
              and here's me...
    what about we shake some juicy fruit
                from the *universal* tree?

  Put away that accent boy,   be yourself!
          Talk about brotherhood   in your own voice....

But to be honest, if I had the choice, I'd be a Jamaican-born   Welshman -

                reggae lovebeat ya bloodclot rastafari froma Nanny Town
                outsida wicked Kingston where da king is from
                Bob Marley I am not so much worthy
                as to gather up the crumbs under your table,
                but when I am able to integrate your redemption fire
                with the higher purposes of the Welsh dragon-bards
              singing like Sunday bells down the long valleys
          of the shadow of death that haunts us all - wherever we are from -
                  I will sing my song:

                    Sing a song of England
                    What will you buy?
                    A Merc, a flat and Sky TV
                    And don't ask why.

                    Entertain ourselves to death
                    Forget who we are
                    Cosmetic surgery is nice
                    It won't leave a scar.

      If   you   do   not   consume -   you   are   nothing!

I consume air -   turning to poison
I consume water -   turning to poison.

I consume   the fruits of the earth
  genetically engineered   by men
  whose wonder and piety have been castrated.

    When I see the companies who want to patent genes... -
when I see the companies who blot out the stars
  with their neon advertising - when I see the soldiers
    who bayonet the monks - when I see the black fingernails
of the man with no family - when I see what I see
            through the mirror

     I consume fire like a fire eater
     I beat fire like a firebeater
     I'm streetwise as a runaway cheetah
     in Camden Town -

but who needs the wisdom of the cynical street
    when we know the wisdom of the beat beyond beyond
               an' further beyond than that?

     Which street are we wise on anyhow?
     Compton, Railton, Piccadilly, Camberwell?
     EC1, W8, N16, SE7?
     All depends on your area right?
     Let's walk together the universal street
     the beat of brotherhood above neighbourhood
     the beat of the blood in every heart
     that knows we've gotta start being
     ourselves before everything else -
     but... who the hell are we?

   We...   me...   we...   me...

My name is Philip Wells   and I'm English   and I'm a man -
       You're not a man, you're a soul   struggling to weave
          together the oppositional   dualities
       of masculine and feminine,   to become whole,
         to be full of radiant power, to pass on
      the knowledge of the light -   and your name -
        Philip Wells - what is your   original name,
          oh boost from the deep?

     I *am* English -   *go back,*   *go back* -

I'm French   I'm a Viking -   *go back,   go back -*
I'm a caveman -   *go back,   go back -*
        I'm a whale   an aphid   a stone!

Go back to the centre.
Where is your home star?
Do you know? Can you remember?
Have you ever listened to the cosmic hiss?

Ask your neighbours to please keep the noise down,
        turn the dimmer switch down on the street glow
                and there you have it -
        as many stars as all the living things that have ever died.

Northern lights brighter than fireworks...
                a meteor crashes and burns in a comet-flash.

What's that?   Oh, that's a Sky TV satellite -
                Does that tell us who we are too?

Ladies and gentlemen, please ignore all previous pronouncements!
There will be endless football, motor racing, celebrity makeover
etcetera etcetera to amuse and anaesthetise you!
There will be endless scenes of violence
to make you appreciate just how lucky you are
that you're not being beaten to pulp right now!
We will try to avoid loving sex wherever possible;
all violent sex gives you the important impression
that the sexes are perpetually at war
which keeps everyone apart and angry
and hungry for those expensive compensatory fixes -
for all these conveniently elusive desires we have
smaller buttons, bigger buttons, bigger screens, smaller screens -
        direct debit? that'll do nicely

invest in cigarettes - a billion Chinese
won't kick that habit -
 keep it all ticking along, ticketiboo -
  the computer network won't crash -
   mother nature can take it, technology'll solve it -
    no such thing as a free meal, lad -
     if everyone did that all at once
      the whole fuckin' place would grind to a halt!
      Bloody do-gooder!

If everyone did   *who everyone   was -*

we don't have words
for that kind of joy.

Identity   is the bridge   we cross   from emptiness
to wholeness: when we reach the light   on the other side,
    we no longer need that bridge,   though we praise and praise
        the wisdom of the genius   who built that bridge.

If everyone did who everyone was -
I know it and I've seen it,
I live it and I say it -

if everyone did who everyone was
mother earth would wake up,
    remember who she was -
    the whole world would change from the inside out -

and your beautiful grandchild will be teaching you
    by firelight   to the sound of the waves   under the stars
all the knowledge of the light - and you'll remember it all -

and fear will dissolve   in the blaze of the sun
and new rains will come and new hearts will bloom   157
and fight with courage against the fearful and the cynical
so new hearts will be free to bloom again

and all because, once, one person listened truly to another
who said   *if everyone did who everyone was -*
and because, soon, everyone began to listen
and because now
everyone does who everyone is
and it's better
than heaven

just because   now

everyone *does*

who
everyone
is

Eastbourne Cliffs

Further, further, Daddy

My little boy takes me further in the sun
Into a miracle where the white pebble
Sits in the chapel of a spring
By the white, white cliffs

And the trickle of the water
Is a rhythm of love:
It is love calling,
This water falling:

Further, further, Daddy

This water falling
On the white pebble
I place now in the secret box
I carry with me forever

For this is the same
White pebble
My son places
On my grave

Further, further, Daddy

And I can hear him clear
As a spring in the white cliff
From the far place
Where I cannot touch him

But where our listening,
Despite all the deep divides,
Splashes us together in the great light
In an everlasting wave of love.

The Revolution Of Revelations

Petals squeezed down the barrels of Kalashnikovs was OK,
But the long division of insurrection's due for correction:
Desperate times call for inspiration out of time, a holy way
To shine the bigbang prayer of the burningsane expansion -

And so recitations of reciprocity erupt with unprecedented ferocity
And the veracity of capacity hearts is the start
Of the end of verbosity and the festival of light in cities
And towns spreads from candle to candle, from heart

To heart, and we can hear the end of fear burning
In the turning spheres of sacred tears of falling light
Too subtle for sense and tense, but second sighting
And the sounding light of it is true - the truth of light -

The time to fight is now, for all those guards to fall -
Bulldozing of the final wall - asleep no more.
We are too bright, too tall, to fall again, too tall
Now we have shrunk upon our knees and score

The rhythmical heat of the heart of ourselves.
Pills we never knew left on darkened shelves
We take now and score the kick of who we truly are:
O holy ghost, you superstar! Never knew how far

The sky stretched through the old bars of who
I thought I was, who I bought I was, the stealing
Of my feelings, little thoughts of me in charge but no,
Now I am the feeling sky breathing round the world your healing.